THE
GODDESS
BIBLE

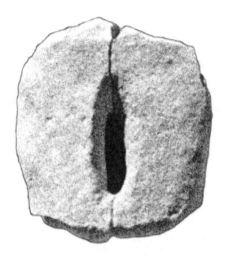

THE
GODDESS
BIBLE

SELECTED, EDITED AND
ANNOTATED BY

ASHRA BALL

Nammu Books
VANCOUVER

Nammu Books
76 – 1146 Pacific Blvd
Vancouver BC V6Z 2X7

info@nammubooks.ca
www.nammubooks.ca
www.ashraball.ca

First published by Nammu Books 2023

THE GODDESS BIBLE

© 2023 Ashra Ball and Nammu Books

Thanks to artist Ama Menec for permission to use her
"Nile Goddess" sculpture in the cover design.
www.amamenec-sculpture.co.uk

Cover design: Jeanne Lewis

ISBN: 978-1-7387395-0-9   (hardcover)
       978-1-7387395-3-0   (paperback)
       978-1-7387395-1-6   (ebook)

For who can understand the mystery
of this god who so loves death
and those who worship him?

TABLE OF CONTENTS

Foundation Scriptures

The Histories

Hymns and Litanies

Wisdom

Prophecy

Appendix

List of Illustrations

Notes

FOREWORD

The discovery of a new scroll jar in a cave at Qumran, allegedly during the Yadin–Bat-Isha excavations in 1995, was kept from the world's press at the time. It was finally announced only in 2007, when the first translations of the texts began to be published. At that point it ignited great interest in the media and among the public. Both the Jordanian government and the Palestine Authority immediately declared a right of interest in the jar and its contents. Those challenges are still proceeding through the courts.

Uniquely among such finds, the scroll jar was intact and still sealed with the original seal. It was found secreted behind a wall of mudbrick, which had been disguised with clay and stones to mimic the appearance of the natural cave structure.

The cave was not one of the four that were the focus of the 1995 excavations, and the jar was said to have been discovered by chance. During a preliminary survey for possible future excavation, the Israeli archaeologist Dr. Yisabel Bat-Isha, then the senior member of the excavation team, apparently chose the cave at random.

On the floor of the cave, she stumbled upon shards of broken clay. This led to her discovery of the wall, which had begun to deteriorate. She was able to dislodge a section of the upper area of the wall, and saw the lip of the sealed scroll jar behind.

When she was interviewed in 2007, Dr. Bat-Isha vividly described her wild elation at that moment. Knowing that any leak to the world's media would cause sensation-seekers to overrun the site, she decided to keep the find secret from the dig team. Instead, she contacted colleagues in the Institute of Archaeology at the Hebrew University, Jerusalem, and the decision was made to smuggle the urn offsite.

What followed was an undercover operation worthy of a thriller. At first, Dr. Bat-Isha worked alone at night to dismantle the wall that concealed the urn. Then several members of the recovery team arrived undercover as new volunteers at the site, smuggling in the equipment needed to crate and bring the scroll jar out of the cave. This task they also undertook by night.

When all was in readiness, Dr. Bat-Isha feigned illness so that her midnight evacuation by air ambulance would be a cover for the removal of the jar. The helicopter landed on Mount Scopus, and the jar was taken to the Institute of Archaeology.

Hadassah Hospital subsequently issued a press release announcing that Dr. Bat-Isha had undergone immediate surgery and that such timely action had saved her life. A small item in the *Jerusalem Post* of July 15th, 1995, reports this, but after so many years it has not been possible to find any member of the team at Qumran who recalls the incident of an emergency air ambulance during the period of the excavations.

Scholars, journalists, and others have challenged this story as improbable for a variety of reasons. Conflicting theories and unfounded speculation about the discovery continue to circulate and are finding a new audience online. (It should perhaps be said here that there is no evidence to support the persistent rumour that the entire cache was hijacked from a secret vault in the Vatican library. Nor is it by any means clear that such a circumstance would account for the well-preserved condition of so many of the documents.)

When pressed on the subject in her interview with the Discovery Channel the year before her death,[1] an unrepentant Dr. Bat-Isha would only say that the story was "substantially true," and that some details had been suppressed or changed in order to protect innocent parties. When asked for the precise location of the cave, and whether the Israeli military had been involved in the retrieval and evacuation of the jar, she failed to answer. The interview ended soon afterwards.

Whatever the truth behind the jar's discovery, the singular importance of its contents cannot be disputed. When the jar was finally opened, under tight laboratory controls, it was found to contain a collection of documents of unprecedented scope and importance, many of them in remarkably good condition.

There can be no question as to the authenticity of the documents. If the condition and variety of the trove were not enough to convince even the most sceptical, the carbon dating puts it beyond doubt. Some parchment scrolls have been dated to 1400 BCE or earlier.

Wherever these documents sprang from, therefore, their historical value is unsurpassed.

N. Anna Dingir
Emeritus Professor of Goddess Religions
SOAS, University of London
Consultant Editor

THE DOCUMENTS

The extraordinary texts now popularly labelled "the Goddess Papers" and "the Rosetta Stone in a jar" detail well over two thousand years of the beliefs, practices, and history of the Goddess-worshippers who lived in the ancient land we call Canaan.

The Goddess religion's High Priestesses and Priestess-Scribes considered themselves under a divine command to keep a written account of themselves and make it accessible to succeeding generations, even as the language they spoke changed with time.

They not only documented their origin myths, sacred liturgies, and history, but also repeatedly translated significant texts into the current vernacular over time. In addition, they must have prioritized the preservation of these records during times of war, displacement, invasion, vandalism, and natural disaster.

In several different languages, on parchment, papyrus and clay tablets, these texts, many of which have been restored and translated during the past 25 years, collectively span two thousand years of history in the land called Canaan.

The result is an astonishing wealth of information, giving us deep insight into the lives of the adherents of the Goddess religion, as well as their interactions with their neighbours on all sides.

Prominent among these neighbours were the people who called themselves Israelites. Over the course of centuries, the Israelite tribes invaded and then spread throughout the areas the Goddess people inhabited, sometimes at war, sometimes in precarious co-existence with them.

From the first incursions in about 1400 BCE and the period of Judges and Kings, through the Babylonian exile, and up to the time of the First Jewish-Roman War, we can now view incidents familiar in Old and New Testament stories from the perspective of the indigenous inhabitants of Jericho and Jezreel and Jerusalem, and lastly even from Qumran.

Not every reader will find the perspective comfortable. But for those who long "to see ourselves as others see us", this collection will be an invaluable gift.

Apparently only a tiny remnant of what was once a comprehensive temple archive, the documents were hidden when they came under threat from the Roman army. Internal evidence indicates that the urn was sealed during the First Jewish-Roman War (66-73CE). It is our extraordinary good fortune that it remained hidden and intact until the present day.

The earliest of the texts are the clay tablets dating from circa 2100 BCE, inscribed in cuneiform in what seems to be a dialect of the language we call Sumerian. A few later clay tablets are inscribed in Akkadian cuneiform. Many of these are broken, but some are relatively well preserved, allowing us to compare the texts with later translations. Several papyrus documents in an early Phoenician script are so deteriorated they may never be read. Many scrolls, both papyrus and parchment, are written in Canaanite, a Semitic dialect previously seen only in monumental inscriptions. These are extremely well preserved, allowing us to read the full text of many letters and records. The most recent documents, dating to the Herodian period, also in excellent condition, are in Aramaic.

There is still an enormous amount to be done. The work of piecing together the broken tablets, teasing apart the fused leaves of the oldest scrolls and then restoring what is written, is ongoing. The Goddess Project has recently received funding that will allow us to implement the latest x-ray, laser, and other technology, and in future years we hope to be able to read many more texts.

Of the documents already restored and translated, we can say that they seem to fall into the following categories: Foundation Scriptures; Historical Records, Letters, and Testimonies; Hymns and Liturgies; Congress Postures; Wisdom and Law; Healing and Medicine; Incantations and Spells; and finally, Prophecy. If, as seems probable, the temples kept records of their fields and storehouses and other such practicalities, they were not important enough to include in this cache.

I have made a selection from the most legible and coherent of the documents so far available. In the Histories, where we have the largest number of documents in very good condition, I have chosen those events that, although written from the perspective of the Goddess-worshippers, will sound familiar to modern readers of the Old and New Testaments.

This book is written for the general public. I have kept footnotes and alternate readings to a minimum. This is not to disguise the fact that there are many uncertain and even disputed readings, but for the sake of narrative flow, I have generally used whatever reading has the best consensus among scholars and left the rest to be fought out in the halls of academia. Any general reader with an interest in such detail can consult the papers that are now being published in the various scholarly journals.

Ashra Ball

Vancouver 2023

A NOTE

ON THE TRANSLATION

A lthough some of the early translation work of the Goddess documents was done by male scholars, it became apparent when preparing for this publication that few if any of those translations were true to the deep meaning of the texts. Even the most educated of scholars, it seems, found it difficult to connect to a sexuality that did not objectify women. Many instances of this occurred, from the simplest to the most outrageous. "Asherah opened the path of pleasure," had become, in one early draft of the text, "Asherah spread her legs." "Great Nammu pleasured Herself," was translated "Great Nammu masturbated."

Whether this kind of insensitivity was produced by awkwardness with the sexual freedom expressed in so many of the texts, or a simple inability to see beyond current sexual attitudes, we did not ascertain. The fact was that to do justice to the cultural worship of and exuberance around sexuality, and especially female sexuality, we had to turn to women scholars entirely.

Even so, we had trouble finding ways to express the free embrace of sexuality as both divine gift and divine attribute. For the adherents of the Goddess religion, the word 'love' also meant 'pleasure'.[2] A woman was never more truly divine than when she was one with the Allmother/Yahu/Asherah in sexual pleasure. The man who helped produce that state bathed in a reflected glory, but apparently did not achieve a *direct* connection to the Lady.

These concepts are so far from our current approach to sex and sexuality that it is difficult to grasp and more difficult to translate. *All* sexual words in the English language fall into two groups—clinical/medical/ latinate or obscene/smutty/vulgar. Or both. Even the word *sex* itself, with all its cognates, has some element of the latter for many English speakers. The conflation of sex with holiness is almost beyond us, and a certain amount of mental adjustment was necessary in order to translate the documents effectively.

For example, the Pleasure People, as they sometimes called themselves, would have been appalled and incredulous that our word *fuck* is so debased as to have become a vile expletive. The word was an impossible choice in any context in the Goddess scriptures, as also are *cunt* and the host of other derogatory terms by which English-language speakers the world over routinely designate their own organs of pleasure.

In the end we chose the word *congress* for the act of sexual union, whether woman with man, woman with woman, man with man, or any combination thereof—for many of which the Goddess people had distinct words, depending on the participants and the orifice. In any case, in some areas we could hardly guess at what position/engagement a particular word indicated, so a general term seemed appropriate.

Another difficulty concerned the terms used for the temple clergy who engaged with worshippers in the sacred pleasure rites. Traditionally, male scholars translating ancient texts, including Old Testament translators for the past 400 years, have used the terms *temple prostitute, male prostitute,* and even *harlot* to designate these people, despite the fact that the word *qadeshtu* derives from the Semitic word *holy* or *sacred*. We felt that such terms could not be divorced from modern connotations that rob sex work and even all sexual activity of dignity. We therefore have used terms more closely related to the intention of the original: *Congress Priestess* and *Congress Priest* as well as *Pleasure Priestess* and *Pleasure Priest*. Such functions were clearly seen as holy, and the holders of these offices were respected and even revered, probably far more than the clergy today.

When it came to words for the human organs of pleasure, the Goddess people had a variety of terms to choose from, and it is still unclear when and why a particular term was used. Here, we have in certain contexts had recourse to the latinate *Vulva* and *Penis,* but in conjunction with other non-clinical words, because the Latin does not at all convey the hallowed affect that the original languages give to these organs. So we use *Holy Vulva* and *Penis Root,* for the sacred is there in every expression used for the former, and the words for *Penis* and *Root* seem to be almost interchangeable. But there are also allegorical terms, and these we have translated literally: *Honey Flower, Goddess Flower, Pleasure Root,* etc.

Given our culture's heavily weighted approach to the question of human sexual pleasure, it seems likely that this will be a difficult leap for the modern reader —

the concept of sexual pleasure as both a sacred gift from and offering to the deity, with the acts and body parts that produce that pleasure wrapped in holiness.

And even after the assault of patriarchal, misogynistic invaders from the south and north, the Goddess people managed to cling onto their sense of the sacred right through to the Herodian period, when the last despairing High Priestess put the cherished remnant of their sacred scriptures into an earthenware jar and walled it up for a future generation to find.

FOUNDATION
SCRIPTURES

In The Time Before Time

In the time before time, before the world, before the
    seasons, before the holy pleasure rites[3]

The Great Allmother Nammu, the Fertile Womb, the
    Pleasure-Loving Vulva
The Allmother Nammu sat in the Great Oneness
She sat in the abyss of emptiness
The Great Allmother Nammu said, I will fill the void with
    my pleasure

The Great Allmother Nammu squatted with Her knees
    wide
She caressed Her Vulva until She was satisfied
Her belly grew big and Her breasts were heavy with milk
Her Holy Vulva spread apart
Great Nammu heaved a heave and cried a cry
She gave birth to Holy Pleasure
She suckled Holy Pleasure at Her breasts
The pleasure grew and spread and filled the void

The Allmother said, I will bring forth my daughters
That they may increase and perpetuate my pleasure

The Great Allmother Nammu squatted with Her knees
    wide
She caressed Her Vulva until She was satisfied
Her belly grew big and Her breasts were heavy with milk
Her Holy Vulva spread apart

1

Great Nammu heaved a heave and cried a cry
She gave birth to Her daughter Yahu
Great Nammu gave birth to the Eight Goddesses and the
    Holy Consorts
She gave birth to spirits and demons
She suckled them with the milk of life
And they conjoined to increase and perpetuate Her
    pleasure

The Great Allmother Nammu said
I will bring forth a Pleasure Garden for my daughters
That they may dwell in perpetual pleasure there

The Great Allmother Nammu squatted with Her knees
    wide
She caressed Her Vulva until She was satisfied
Her belly grew big and Her breasts were heavy with milk
Her Holy Vulva spread apart
Great Nammu heaved a heave and cried a cry
She gave birth to the Great Above and the Great Below
She gave birth to the Earth between
She gave birth to the Dark and the Light
She gave birth to the sacred mountain and the lowlands
    and the waters
She gave birth to the sacred tree and the plants, the
    grasses, the flowers
She suckled them with the milk of life
They conjoined with pleasure
They grew and spread and filled the horizons

The Great Allmother Nammu said

I will bring forth the multitude
That they may live in my Pleasure Garden
That they may increase and perpetuate my pleasure

The Great Allmother Nammu squatted with Her knees
    wide
She caressed Her Vulva until She was satisfied
Her belly grew big and Her breasts were heavy with milk
Her Holy Vulva spread apart
Great Nammu heaved a heave and cried a cry
She gave birth to the wisdom serpents
She gave birth to the creatures of wing and fin and foot
She gave birth to every living creature
She suckled Her creatures with the milk of life
And they conjoined to increase and perpetuate Her
    pleasure

The Allmother said to Her daughter Yahu
She said to the Eight Goddesses
See what I have birthed!
From Oneness I have brought the many
Out of my pleasure I have brought the multitude
I have birthed a Pleasure Garden for you
I have birthed the Great Above and the Great Below
I have birthed the Earth between
I have birthed darkness and light
I have birthed earth and sky
I have birthed the sacred mountain and lowlands and
    waters
I have birthed the sacred tree and the plants, the grasses
    and flowers

I have birthed the wisdom serpents
I have birthed creatures of wing and fin and foot

I have birthed them all

All this I have done from my Vulva pleasure
I have filled the Oneness with Many
Let them live in my Pleasure Garden without care
Let them undertake the Pleasure Congress
Let the garden be filled with their Vulva pleasures
Let their pleasures rise and enrich my dreams

The Great Allmother Nammu squatted with Her knees
    wide
She caressed Her Vulva until She was satisfied
But Her belly did not swell nor Her breasts grow heavy
The Great Allmother Nammu had finished Her tasks
Allmother Nammu lay down with Her arm under Her
    head
Great Nammu closed Her eyes and slept.

THE COMING OF THE PLEASURES

The Allmother's sleep was disturbed
Great Nammu's sleep was fitful
The people did not know the Allmother
They wandered in Her sacred Pleasure Garden
They did not know the Allmother
The people did not send Her pleasure offerings
The Allmother did not dream of the people

Go to the women, Great Yahu
Take them our gifts
Take them the gift of Holy Worship
Teach them the sacred pleasure rites
Teach them the Art of Congress
Teach them the Kissing of the Honey Flower
Teach them the Stroking of the Root
Teach them the Softened Vulva
Teach them the Erect Tree
Teach them Mounting the Mountain

Take them the Holy Pleasure Tools
Take them the sacred *unna* beads
Take them the golden *urra* rod
Take them the pleasure glove
Take them the sacred herbs
Take them the *arra* oil and the *nani'a* oil
Take them the *murtu'u* oil
Take them the thirteen Pleasure Postures

5

Teach them the *bunu* posture
Teach them the *char* posture
Teach them the *atana and utana* posture
Teach them the *turm* posture
Teach them the *ashur* posture
Teach them the *setaru* posture
Teach them the *ha'ow* posture
Teach them the *bao'u and ortha* posture
Teach them the *standing arba* posture
Teach them the *naruju* posture
Teach them the *upara* posture
Teach them the *timun* posture
Teach them the *panj* posture

Take them the Sacred Shrine
Take them the hill shrine
Take them the tree shrine
Take them the sacred pillar
Take them the offering bed
Take them the altar

Let the people make pleasure offerings
Let them send pleasure to the Allmother's dreams
Let Her dream of Her people

Yahu will go to the people
She will bring the Allmother's gifts to the people

THE CONSORT

A Holy Consort was envious
Elohi was envious
A consort of the Eight Goddesses was jealous
Elohi was jealous

Elohi said to his brothers
The people are sending pleasure offerings to the
  Allmother's dreams
They send kissing the Vulva Flower
They send stroking the Penis Root
They send mounting the mountain
They send watering the womb

They do not know us
They do not send us worship
They do not make offerings to us
Only to Great Nammu, the Allmother

The consort was angry
Elohi was angry
He said, why do they send offerings to Great Nammu
The Allmother who is asleep?
Why do they pleasure Her dreams?
They send nothing to us
They send nothing to the consort-gods
They offer only to Great Nammu who is asleep

I will send the people an omen
I will send them a warning

I will send flood and famine
So that they know us
I will send disaster
I will send disease
I will destroy Great Nammu's Pleasure Garden
I will drive them out of the Pleasure Garden
The people will know my anger
They will know that I am a jealous god
They will make offerings to me
They will send smoke offerings
They will make sacrifice offerings
They will make blood offerings
I am a jealous god

Elohi said I will send rain
I will send a flood to the Pleasure Garden
I will cause the rivers to rise
I will make of the Pleasure Garden a sea
There will be no house, no sheepfold
There will be no place for them
Until they make offerings to me
Until they offer blood

Elohi said I will send earthquake
The sacred mountain will vomit fire
I will hide the sun
There will be no light for them
Until they make offerings to me
Until they offer me their sheep

Elohi said I will send disease upon them
I will send pain and disfigurement

There will be no ease for them
No comfort
Until they make sacrifice to me
Until they offer me their children

The rains came without ceasing
The waters of earth rose
The rivers rose
The Allmother's garden was flooded
There was no house, no sheepfold
There was no place for the people

The earth shook and trembled
Fire reached towards the heavens
Smoke hid the sun
There was no light for the people

The people became ill
They were in pain
Their bodies shrivelled and swelled
Their suffering was great

The people wept and wailed
Elohi is angry with us
The Pleasure Garden is cursed
We must leave the Pleasure Garden
They fled to the eight directions
They fled to the mountains
They fled to the caves
The people were lost and dismayed
They were sick and hungry
They forgot the pleasure offerings for Allmother Nammu

They made sacrifice to the consort-god
They made smoke and blood offerings to Elohi
They sacrificed their children for the bloodlust of Elohi

They neglected the kissing of the Vulva Flower
They neglected the stroking of the Penis Root
They neglected mounting the mountain
There was no watering of the womb

Great Nammu's sleep was disturbed
There were no pleasure offerings in Her dreams

Yahu looked to the earth
Yahu saw the suffering of the people
She was angry with the consort Elohi
Why have you sent disaster to the Allmother's Pleasure
    Garden?
Why have you made Her people suffer?
Why do you seek blood offerings?
Why do you ask of them blood sacrifice, the blood of their
    children?

Elohi was shamed before the Eight Goddesses
He was shamed before the consorts
He made no answer to Holy Yahu

This is the Great Lady's will
Nammu has not birthed you from Her sacred Vulva
You are neither son nor lover
You are not of the family of gods
You are no longer our consort, Elohi
None will enact the sacred pleasure rites with you

Your root will not enter our sacred Vulvas
Your emission will not water our wombs
You are cast out forever from our abode

You will travel the empty worlds fondling your root alone
You will wander between heaven and earth
A bar between the Great Lady Nammu and the people
Those who offer blood sacrifice to you
Will no longer make pleasure offerings to the Lady
Great Nammu will not dream of them
They will be cursed
They will live without joy
They will be driven out of the lands
They will find nowhere to build their blood altars
They will wander Great Nammu's earth
Seeking a place
Finding none
Their fear and suffering will be your sustenance
So you will increase their fear and suffering
You will drink their blood sacrifices to no avail
They will be cursed

Until the day they remember the Lady
Until they remember Great Nammu
Until they make love offerings again to Great Nammu
So that She sees them in Her dreams

YAHU'S GIFTS

The Allmother's sleep was disturbed
Great Nammu's sleep was fitful
The Allmother's Pleasure Garden was a ruin
The people had fled to the eight directions
They were suffering and grieving
They wandered without solace
Their torment reached the ears of Heaven

Send to the women, Great Yahu
Ease their suffering
Send to the women
Send them the gifts

Send them the High Priestess
Send them the Congress Priestess
Send them the Priestess Healer
Send them the Prophecy Priestess
Send them the Sacrifice Priestess
Send them the Castration Priestess

Send them Prophecy
Send them the wisdom snakes
Send them the homa smoke
Send them the incantations
Send them the mysteries
Send them the teaching stories
Send them the sacred circles
....[4]

12

Send them the Calendar[5]
Send them the thirteen moons
Send them the three weeks
Send them the days

Send them the Holy Days
Send them Great Nammu Day
Send them the Pleasure Festival
Send them Lady Day
Send them the Dark Moon Days

Send them Healing
Send them the holy touch
Send them the laying on of hands
Send them the nectar of Vulva-Blood-and-Honey
Send them the balm of Vulva-Blood-and-Salt
Send them the healing herbs
Send them the scented oil
....
Send them music
Send them dance
Send them song
Send them the worship hymns
Send them the harp and flute
Send them the tambour and drum

Send them dried reeds
Send them the weaving of baskets
Send them the spinning of yarn
Send them knitting and dyeing

Send them the kiln
Send them fired clay
Send them painted clay
Send them oil jars

....

Send them wrought metal
Send them beaten gold
Send them the melting of metal
Send them fire vessels

Send them Numbers
Send them counting and reckoning
Send them weighing and measuring

....

Send them the written word
Send them the pressed clay
Send them the pointed stylus
Send them the Priestess-Scribe

Send them the Holy City
Send them the Sacred Precinct
Send them the Built Temple
Send them the Congress Hall
Send them the Altar Bed

Send all the gifts of Great Nammu to the daughters

Yahu will send to the daughters
She will send Nammu's gifts to the daughters

ASHERAH'S BIRTH

The Great Lady Yahu went to the Sacred Mountain
She lit the *homa* incense and called Her daughter Asherah
    to Her womb
Yahu sang Asherah's name to Her daughter

Yahu took a consort from among the sons of women
She taught him Her daughter's name
She said to him, Pleasure me so that my daughter may
    come to the world through my Holy Vulva
I will send her to my people beside the sacred river to
    teach them my gifts and my worship

The Great Lady Yahu's consort performed the ablutions
    and the sacrifice
He chewed cardamom seeds to sweeten his breath
He perfumed himself with myrrh
He painted his lips with the sacred *nani'a* pleasure
    ointment and his Sacred Root with *arra*
He came to the Sanctuary
He knelt beside the Lady on Her bed of cedar and
    perfumed linen
He recited Her holy names
He kissed Her breasts and Her Holy Vulva

The Lady opened Her Goddess Flower to him, she
    opened the pathway to Her Womb
The Lady said, Give me the Pleasure of the Conjoining,
    my consort

The consort toyed with Her in the Root Kiss for a night
and a day[6]
The Goddess Yahu sang the song of holy joy
The Great Lady Yahu blessed the consort, saying, You are
worthy. Water my Holy Womb and let us send our
pleasure to the Allmother so that my daughter
Asherah may come forth
Their pleasure was pleasing to Great Nammu

Lady Yahu called Asherah by name and Asherah came
forth from Her Holy Vulva
The Great Lady Yahu gave the wisdom snakes into
Asherah's keeping
She said to Asherah
Go to my people by my holy river
Let them build you a house by the river and live there
among them
Take them my gifts and teach them my worship so that
they may thrive again

THE HOLY CITY

The Lady Asherah came to the sacred river
She came with the wisdom serpents given to her by her
    Mother the Lady Yahu
The Lady Asherah called to the people
She called to the women, the men
She called to the *hur* and the *palla*
She called to the *bral* and the *shen*[7]
She called to all the people

She said to them, I am sent by my holy Mother, the Lady
    Yahu, to bring you Her gifts and teach you Her arts
Asherah said, Build me a house here by the sacred river,
    so that I may live among you and teach you the best
    worship of the Allmother
Asherah said, I will teach you the arts and learning sent to
    you by my Mother the Lady Yahu

The people gathered from all the land
The women, the men, the *hur* and the *palla*, the *bral* and
    the *shen* came to the sacred river
They made mud bricks and fashioned them into walls
They made a roof of palm leaves and woven reeds
They made a door of olive wood
They sealed the walls inside and out with fine clay
They painted the clay with sacred purple so that all would
    know this was the house of the Lady

Asherah said, At Yahu's command I will found a city

Asherah said, I will found a worship temple so that you
may come together on the Holy Days and offer your
pleasure to Great Nammu the Allmother

The Lady Asherah laid out the temple where the people,
the women and men, the *hur* and the *palla*, the *bral*
and the *shen* could gather and perform the worship
rites together

She laid out gardens and baths for the enjoyment of the
people, the women and men, the *hur* and the *palla*,
the *bral* and the *shen*, who would come to worship at
Great Nammu's shrine

She laid out an approach to the great spring so that the
people, the women and men, the *hur* and the *palla*,
the *bral* and the *shen* could collect pure water

She laid out a wall around the city, to keep the Sacred
Precinct holy

She ordered gates of polished olive wood to be hung, to
enclose it

The people, the women and men, the *hur* and the *palla*, the
bral and the *shen* built the temple that Asherah laid
out

They built the gardens and the baths

They built the approach to the great spring

They built the wall to enclose the city in holiness

They hung gates of polished olive wood

Asherah called the city Yah'riho, which means, Yahu's
Command

Asherah carried the wisdom snakes into the Holy City,
into the house of purple

She gave the people all the gifts of Holy Mother Yahu
She taught the people the ways of love
She taught the songs of worship, she taught the sacred
rites
She taught all the wisdom of the Lady Yahu
We call the city Yah'riho the Holy City, Yah'riho the
Beautiful

DUMUZZI'S MANOEUVRES

Dumuzzi[8] yearned to taste the sacred fig
The sacred fig forbidden to men
O my Lady, O my Sweet Beloved, O my Queen
Give me to eat of the sacred fig
Let me understand the mystery

Innasherah[9] held the fig tight in her closed hand
She did not give Dumuzzi the fig
The sacred fig is not for you, Dumuzzi
The fig's secret is gifted to me by my Holy Mother Yahu
The sacred fig is not for you

How will I please the Allmother
If I do not know the Divine Secret?

Dumuzzi dipped his hands in the *arra* pleasure oil
He knelt beside the Lady Innasherah
He anointed her hair with the *arra* pleasure oil
He slowly stroked Innasherah with the *arra* pleasure oil
He pinched her ears
He patted her eyelids and forehead
He brushed her mouth and cheeks
He fondled her neck
He rubbed her shoulders
He pressed her arms
He squeezed her hands and every finger
He pummelled her thighs
He tapped her knees

He stroked her feet and every toe
He caressed her breasts
He nipped her nipples
He kneaded her back and her buttocks
He circled her belly
He anointed her Honey Flower
He massaged the *arra* oil deep for a night and a day
Innasherah's pleasure sighs filled the Sanctuary

O my Lady, give me to eat of the sacred fig
Let me know the wisdom
But Innasherah held the fig tight in her closed hand
Dumuzzi, the sacred fig is not for you

How will I please the Allmother
If I do not know the Divine Secret?

My pleasure has not reached the Allmother, Dumuzzi
My pleasure has not entered Great Nammu's dreams

Dumuzzi anointed his lips with the *nani'a* holy ointment
His tongue he dipped in the *nani'a* pleasure ointment
He took the *bao'u* posture before the Lady Innasherah
He kissed the sacred Goddess Flower of Innasherah
His tongue toyed with her Holy Vulva for a night and a
        day
Lady Innasherah's pleasure cries filled the Sacred Grove

O my Lady, give me to eat of the sacred fig
Let me understand the wisdom
But Innasherah held the fig in her closed hand
Dumuzzi, the sacred fig is not for you

How will I please the Allmother
If I do not know the Divine Secret?

My pleasure has not reached the Allmother, Dumuzzi
My pleasure has not entered Great Nammu's dreams

Dumuzzi took up the sacred *unna* beads
He took up the pleasure chain
He anointed the beads with *murtu'u* oil
With *murtu'u* oil he anointed Innasherah's aperture
He pressed the *unna* chain into her holy anus
He withdrew the *unna* beads one by one
Each time Innasherah sighed with pleasure
Her sighs touched the clouds of the Great Above

O my Lady, give me to eat of the sacred fig
Let me discover the secret wisdom
But Innasherah held the fig in her hand
Dumuzzi, the sacred fig is not for you

How will I please the Allmother
If I do not know the Divine Secret?

My pleasure has not reached the Allmother, Dumuzzi
My pleasure has not entered Great Nammu's dreams

Dumuzzi took the *utana* posture
Dumuzzi anointed his Goddess Root with *arra* oil
His Pleasure Shaft he readied for Innasherah
He lifted Innasherah with his left arm
Innasherah he raised into the *atana* posture
His right hand he dipped in *nani'a* oil

22

He stroked Innasherah's Sacred Vulva with *nani'a* oil
He parted the mouth of her Honey Flower with his fingers
He rubbed his Goddess Root against the Holy Lips
For a night and a day
Innasherah moaned her pleasure
Her pleasure alerted the Great Above
Innasherah cried her pleasure so that the Eight Goddesses
    drew near with joy

O my Lady, give me to eat of the sacred fig
Let me know the wisdom
But Innasherah held the fig in her hand
Dumuzzi, the sacred fig is not for you

How will I please the Allmother
If I do not know the Divine Secret?

My pleasure has not reached the Allmother, Dumuzzi
My pleasure has not entered Great Nammu's dreams

Dumuzzi adopted the *setaru* posture
He invited Innasherah into the *setaru* posture
The *unna* chain he pressed into her sacred aperture
He drew out the holy beads one by one
Dumuzzi's Goddess Root he pressed into her Holy Vulva
Each time he drew back he pressed forward again
For a night and a day
Innasherah trembled with holy joy
Innasherah cried her pleasure into the dreams of the
    Allmother
Great Nammu's dreams filled with Holy Pleasure
Her blessings dropped like rain on the world

O my Lady, give me to eat of the sacred fig
Let me know the wisdom

How will I please the Allmother
If I do not know the Divine Secret?

Innasherah turned on Dumuzzi the drowsy eyes of love
Her hand was like the softened Vulva
She gave the sacred fig into Dumuzzi's grasp
Put it into your mouth whole, Dumuzzi mine
Taste the sacred fig whole
Do not bite the sacred fig in two

Dumuzzi disobeyed his Queen's command
He yearned for the wisdom forbidden to men[10]
He bit the sacred fig in two

Innasherah repented of her softness
Her eyes burned and her heart hardened against Dumuzzi
You have done ill, Dumuzzi
This Holy Wisdom is not for men
None who gain the secret can live
Innasherah commanded her women
Take Dumuzzi out of my presence
Take him out of the Sanctuary
Let his blood fertilize the fields[11]

The Histories

RAHAVA AND YANAB

*Entered into the record by the hand of the Scribe-Historian Dolaan,
this Tanrit Day of Allmother Week of the Upara Moon in the 8th
year of the reign of The High Priestess Queen Yanoeh.*

I n the eighth year of the reign of High Priestess Yanoeh
of Yarosaleem, a warlike tribe began invading and pillaging cities among the Amurru east of the Sacred River,
alarming all the cities of Canaan. In Upara Moon the tribe
crossed the sacred river and attacked Holy Yariho. The
Lady Yanoeh had word of the attack, and sent a runner to
the Lady Rahava, High Priestess of Yariho. But before the
runner returned, Yanab, a young Congress Priestess of the
Yariho temple, arrived in Yarosaleem. It was Fera Day of
Allmother Week.

Yanab was distraught and ill, her clothes stained in
blood and filth, carrying a baby wrapped in one of the
sacred tapestries from the temple there. The infant was
dead, but in Yanab's extreme distress she could hardly be
persuaded to let anyone take it from her.

She had news for the Lady Yanoeh about the fate of
the High Priestess Rahava and the city, and gave the
following report.

The Lady Rahava learned from her scouts that the
marauding tribe had camped close to Yariho, just across
the Sacred River. She sent emissaries to them, enquiring
as to their intentions. Her emissaries did not return.
Rahava and the King were gravely concerned, for though

the city was well fortified, it had only the king's household guard as a standing army.

Soon after, on Asherah Day of Daughter Week, two male strangers came to the temple and asked to perform the rites with Congress Priestesses. After the sacrament they confessed that they were scouts from the camp of the strange tribe, assigned by their warlord to spy out the land and the city.

They themselves worshipped Asherah as Nut. They said that many among the raiders did so, but only in secret, for their leader Yishwa was a harsh and pitiless man who worshipped a God of Death. This man hated Our Lady of Love and had forbidden worship of Her in any form among his tribe, for fear of angering his own god.

These men brought to Rahava a terrible warning. The invaders had a demon-device that would destroy the city's ramparts and even drive the inhabitants mad. So dangerous was this device that the invaders themselves were forbidden to go nearer to it than two thousand cubits. All the priests who had the honour of carrying the device were deaf and had to be frequently replaced when they died.

The army would attack Yariho carrying this device within a short time.

Worse, surrender was not possible. Yishwa would not be satisfied merely to conquer. He had already instructed his army that the God of Death commanded them, when they entered the city, to destroy it utterly, to kill every living thing, women, children, men and animals, without mercy. They were even to uproot and burn the gardens and trees, so that no living evidence would remain of those who worshipped the Goddess of Love.

The scouts wept and said they could do nothing to prevent this certain slaughter, but they hoped to save the High Priestess Rahava and her daughters and all who sheltered in her household at the time of attack. They would tell their leader Yishwa that Rahava had helped them escape when they were in danger, and that they had promised her safety as a reward. They gave her a red flag to hang from the temple portico as a sign. Then they prostrated themselves weeping before the sacred Asherah icon, begging the Goddess's pardon for what they could not help.

The wisdom snakes warned of great evil. Rahava summoned the king and told him of the warning. They alerted the people within and without the walls.

The women from the houses and farms outside the gates came in to shelter with their households and animals. The people collected and distributed axes, knives, scythes, and other tools.

Early on the morning of Lat, the king's scouts came with the news that a large army of the invaders was crossing at the ford. All who were fit, women and men, stationed themselves around the inner wall and most heavily at the gates, which were closed and barricaded. Infants and young children were collected in the marketplace, but many afterwards escaped to run to their mothers by the wall.

The king's household guard, women and men, were set to patrol the upper ramparts.

When the invaders arrived near the city, instead of attacking they turned at a distance of three hundred cubits and began circling the city, shouting and blowing rams' horns. They followed behind a strange device on a sled. This circling continued throughout the day, while the Goddess's people waited for the attack.

But there was no attack before nightfall, and fires showed that the invaders had withdrawn some distance and set up camp. The sentries on the ramparts reported that armed guards had camped outside each of the city gates, and that escape was now impossible.

The people did not return to their homes. Some slept by the walls, some on the roofs of the houses built against the walls, to be in readiness for a dawn assault. The Lady Rahava went to the temple Sanctuary and asked the Goddess for wisdom, but she did not receive an answer.

There was no dawn assault. Again the next morning, the invaders marched around the walls, this time at fifty cubits distance, still following the strange device. Again they shouted and blew horns. Dust fell from the upper mud brick portion of the walls, sometimes choking those who waited below. (The walls of Yariho being stone-built seven cubits high, and above that another four cubits of mud brick.)

Again as the sun set the invaders withdrew to camp at a distance. That night the people did not sleep, but stayed wakeful, fearful that the invaders meant to launch a night attack.

On Izadeh the army marched closer. Dirt and pebbles from the earthen upper part of the wall were now falling on the roofs and the heads of the citizens, and once the king's soldiers cried anxiously that the earthen ramparts were trembling as if in an earthquake. Children plugged their ears and ran screaming to their mothers' skirts, and many of the people fell to weeping, they knew not why.

That night the campfires were so close that those within the walls could hear the shouts of the sentries. It was the Eve of Lady Day, and the people were exhausted with fear, hunger, and fatigue. The king ordered that one half of the patrols should go and eat and rest at home for one watch, and the remainder on Lady Day, for surely not even a barbarian could attack on the Goddess's Holy Day.

But as the people returned to their posts at dawn, the watchers above called down that the army was approaching again. This time they marched under the shadow of the walls, and in close formation. The noise they made was deafening, piercing, and inside the walls the people dropped their weapons to stop their ears.

Then a great roar blasted the air, worse than the loudest thunder. All the upper section of the wall, the earthworks above the stone, disappeared, and the king's household guard with it. A cloud of dust rose up, hiding the sun. Bricks, stones and hard-packed earth fell down on those within, injuring many. But the greater part fell outwards, and the invaders, with a shout of victory, were able to climb up the mounds of fallen brick.

They stood screaming for victory atop the stone wall that was all that now encircled the city, no higher than seven cubits. They jumped down onto the roofs, picking up fallen bricks and hurling them down on the heads of the people. Many were wounded and many killed—women, men, and children—and great was the distress.

No one inside could climb up to them—anyone who tried was struck with so many bricks that they fell instantly in their own blood. Soon the invaders jumped down upon the Great Lady's people and began the slaughter in earnest with sword and spear. Their numbers were overwhelming, and many of the Goddess's people died within the first hour of the breach. It was soon clear that the invaders would show no mercy, accept no surrender, for they killed anyone who offered it, and with cries of triumph they gutted the wounded where they fell.

Finally, the Lady Rahava led a large group of survivors on a difficult retreat, through homes and lanes, till they had regained the temple. There the High Priestess laid spells on the street and the door, then hung the red flag from the portico. All those gathering within trembled in fear and horror, for who could know if such a cruel and merciless people would keep the promise that their scouts had given to Rahava?

They sheltered for a night and a day while the sounds of destruction, the victory cries of the invaders, the screams of people or animals, and the smell of burning rose without. The animals within the temple also began to scream, and for fear that their cries would alert the bloodthirsty army without, Rahava took up the sacrifice knife and without ritual slaughtered them.

The two men did come back and led away Rahava and all those who had sheltered in the temple, but whether they were taken to the invaders' camp or slaughtered in their turn, no one can know.

Yanab was the smallest of the Congress Priestesses. Before leaving, Rahava removed the pleasure tools, oint-

ments and herbs from the Sacred Chest, packing them
along with one tapestry of the Timun Congress, and the
wisdom serpents, to take with her.

Rahava settled Yanab into the empty chest, saying she
would spell the chest and the door of the Holy Sanctuary
so that the invaders would not see or open it. She commanded Yanab to make her way to Yarosaleem when she
could, and tell the Lady Yanoeh of the destruction of the
Holy City. She kissed the Congress Priestess Yanab with
tears of grief and gave her a sacrifice knife, two waterskins
and the last of their dried dates. She gave her the Lady's
blessing and closed her into the chest in darkness. Then
all departed with the strangers and were not seen again.

Yanab stayed inside the sacred chest, listening while
the invaders smashed the outer temple door and came
inside the Great Hall. She smelled smoke and heard shouts
and the sounds of breaking ceramic and wood, then loud
cries of triumph at the thunder of stone falling on stone.
But the door of the Holy Sanctuary was not breached, and
soon enough there was silence in the outer temple. She
waited until her waterskins were empty, but how long that
was she didn't know.

When at last Yanab dared to come out of the Sacred
Receptacle, it was near evening, but she didn't know of
which day. She opened the door of the Sanctuary and saw
the temple destroyed. Asherah's Bed had been broken, the
cedar branches burnt to ash and the pure linens scorched
and blackened and foully defiled. The smell of excrement
and urine mixed with smoke choked her to sickness. The
great image of Our Holy Lady lay shattered under its
plinth. The icons were broken. The tapestries and mosaics

of the Sacred Congresses were desecrated and defiled with shit, piss and fire.

All the gold and silver—the worship and dedication offerings, statues and bowls and pleasure rods, were gone.

Yanab stumbled over a woman's head near the outer door, the long hair tangled with blood and earth, the mouth wide and black with dried blood, and eyes staring. In place of one ear there was only a hole black with blood; the other ear was ragged and frayed where earrings had been torn out of the flesh. One tiny earring remained.

The Congress Priestess knew only one of the Lady's death benedictions, which she was not anointed to recite; nevertheless, she knelt and recited it for the dead woman. She found a small unbroken icon of The Lady with Spread Vulva. She whispered a prayer for permission and took it up, along with the cleanest of the Congress panels. Tying these in a bundle with her knife and waterskins, she stepped through the broken doorway into the street.

Then she saw the destruction of the Holy City Yariho and wished her eyes could not see. The bodies of the dead lay where they had fallen, the children's bodies no less mutilated than their parents'. Houses were blackened from fire. The gardens had been torn up; trees hacked down. The pools were choked with debris and bodies. The market square was in ruins, the children massacred, every-thing smashed and broken.

Animals, too, had been slaughtered throughout the city, and lay in pools of blood. Some were only hamstrung; others were still alive in spite of being stabbed or burnt. These screamed piteously until Yanab was able to dispatch them with the sacrifice knife. This was a difficult task, as many struggled and resisted.

When she went to the spring to wash, it was blocked with the body of a young man she had worshipped with only the week previously. She dragged the body clear and bathed without the recitation because she could not remember it. She filled her waterskins, then rinsed her robe and put it on wet and still bloodied.

As she made her way through the rubble towards the West Gate she saw only dead bodies, until she heard cries from inside a house. She entered through the smashed doorway and found a woman lying on the floor, her legs wide, her robe open. Her breasts and stomach and thighs were scratched and bruised with strange blood-soaked abrasions. Her Vulva was torn and bleeding, and one of her cheeks was slit open; her mouth was gaping and choked with dried blood. There were flies in clouds. The woman's body still had the rhythm of the Goddess breath, but her own breath and heart were stopped. She had probably died only a little earlier.

The screaming came from the baby lying against her left breast. The infant's chest was black with bruises. It stopped screaming and stared at Yanab before beginning to wail again. Yanab could not comfort her. There was no food that had not been defiled, stamped into the earth or worse. She gave the baby water from the end of her finger, but the infant could not swallow. She wrapped the baby in the sacred panel she had brought from the temple, and tied it around her own body, and the infant fell silent. She went back into the street with the baby.

All the people she saw throughout the city, women, children, and men, were dead. She recognized many of the bodies, although some were mutilated beyond recognition. She did not see that of the Lady Rahava or any of those who had been led off by the two men. She saw no invader's body, though she knew some few had been killed.

She was afraid to call for the living in case some of the invaders still were within the city. All the houses had been broken into or burnt or both. Blood was settled between the paving stones; thick clouds of flies rose up as she passed.

Yanab found the Yarosaleem gate still barricaded. She went to the East gate, which the invaders had smashed and burnt. She could see the smoke of small fires rising from the invaders' encampment at a little distance and heard the sounds of drunken rejoicing.

She crouched inside an empty water butt and comforted the infant while night fell. Then she crept out of the gate and made her way through the shadows around the fallen walls of the city. She thought it must be Devi or Asherah Day of Mother Week because the moon was swollen. The moonlight showed how the soldiers of the king's household had been trapped as the wall fell, their arms and legs sticking up like naked tree branches from the rubble of dirt and mud bricks. She met no one living. She set out on the road up to Yarosaleem.

She did not know how long it had taken her to reach Yarosaleem, nor whether she had found food on her way. The infant she carried was dead at least two days. Yanab herself was very weak and sick, but she would not rest until she had told the news to the High Priestess, in the presence of the Scribe-Historian Dolaan.

When she had told the history of the destruction of the Holy City Yariho, Yanab died.

BAHLOUL AND SHILAH

Recorded by the Priestess Scribe Dalit on Izadeh of Daughter Week of Panjeh, in the 12th year of the reign of the High Priestess Ashtara

I n the ninth year of Queen Ashtara's reign, the Elohists—long the most troublesome of all our subject peoples—nominated as their leader a brute giant of exceeding strength named Shimshin. This was a man already known to us for his regular visits to the temples in Timnath and Ashdod, where he was often disruptive— impatient for his own pleasure offering and ignoring his obligation to the Lady. Our Congress Priestesses tried in vain to teach him the correct rites. They reported that he was a braggart about his strength and acumen, recounting his triumphs over his fellow Elohists in various schemes. In truth he seemed a blundering fool whom anyone could outwit.

Shimshin was given to fits of rage in which he ran rampant with whatever weapon he found to hand, and would come down on a village and kill any man he saw for the sake of a rope belt or gold ring or linen robe. The Amalekites and others were perpetually complaining and sending to beg us to deal with him. But though the Elohists called him their leader, Shimshin never came when summoned to confer with Queen Ashtara, and if we had brought him by force, there was no knowing what he would do.

One day, coming into the temple at Timnath, it happened that Shimshin was invited by a new young Congress

Priestess who did not know of him. Shilah, daughter of the Priestess Rahona, worshipped with him, and his offering with her was so pleasing to the Goddess that Shimshin fell in love with Shilah. He swore that he would marry her and take her back to his people as his consort.

He returned a week later with a kid as offering for her parents, and when those at the temple told him that Shilah was a temple devotee consecrated to the Goddess and the pleasure rites, he became enraged, shouting that no one should worship with her save himself.

He ripped the screaming goat apart with his bare hands, defiling a tapestry with its scattered blood, then tore off one of the gold handles of the temple door and with it broke the skulls of two congregants before fleeing.

He came back on the following day. It happened to be a festival day for Timnath, and all were at worship. Shimshin set fire to the temple enclosure, its olive groves and vineyards. Several large stacks of harvested grain were burnt, and the flock of lambs and kids in the paddock.

The smoke and the terrified bleating of the animals, whose pelts were aflame, alerted the celebrants in the temple, and they rushed out naked and unarmed, dazed with the sacred herb. Shimshin killed a worshipper and our Congress Priest Danan, who tried to intervene, before again fleeing.

Trackers soon set off in pursuit, and after three days found that he was hiding in a cave above an Elohist valley. Two of them stayed to watch there while the third took the news to the Priestess Yadol of Timnath. The Lady summoned her consort to take a squad of soldiers down to arrest Shimshin.

When Thimanto and his warriors arrived, the trackers told him what they had discovered: the cave had a long, narrow entrance passage that only one man could enter at a time. An armed man with Shimshin's strength, and the advantage of being within, could outlast a hundred men, killing them one after the other.

Thimanto went to the Elohists living in the valley and told them to bind Shimshin and bring him down, or their own fields and flocks would be laid waste.

The Elohists went up and brought him down bound with what looked like strong ropes, but as soon as he was led to Thimanto he burst these false bonds, and with a knife he had concealed under his arm, quickly killed a man and wounded three more. He ran back to the cave. When Thimanto returned the next day with a larger squad, the cave was empty, and the trackers had lost him.

After that we heard of him once or twice visiting the Congress Priestesses at the temple in Gaza. It was two years before Shimshin came to Timnath again and this time, his eye fell on a woman named Bahloul—by the Goddess's will, the sister of the Congress Priest Danan whom Shimshin had killed in his rampage.

Shimshin demanded congress worship with her. Bahloul refused. When she saw that this rejection seemed to fire him with determination (such being the sort of man he was), however, she made up her mind to avenge her brother on him and see him punished before the Lady.

Bahloul spoke to the Priestess Yadol and they forged a plan for his punishment.

The next time Shimshin approached her, Bahloul promised congress with him only if, as a test of his strength, he would let her tie him with ropes and could break free. She showed him a few thin ropes, and he agreed to the test. These he easily broke and then demanded congress with her.

Bahloul, pretending admiration for his strength, engaged him in *Setaru*. Shimshin had great pleasure, and soon returned to Timnath. The second time, she bound him with thicker ropes, and again he escaped the bonds easily. Bahloul had served in the temple and knew well the Lady's favourite pleasure tricks and toys, and Shimshin became besotted with her, returning again and again.

She always insisted on a test of strength, and each time rewarded him with a new posture, a new device. The temple weaver braided ropes that were secretly flawed and weak. Bahloul marvelled as each time with brute strength Shimshin broke free, and his braggadocio was much increased by this proof of his strength. So was his love for Bahloul.

Then the temple weaver asked for a thick lock of Bahloul's hair. He produced a cord of leather that seemed to be a braid of hair. This was soaked in water. Promising Shimshin a congress pleasure unlike any he had experienced before if he allowed himself to be tied with her own hair, Bahloul tied the wet rope tightly around his testicles and his wrists. Then she bade him sit while she danced for him.

As she danced the leather dried and shrank. Shimshin grew nervous and began to struggle to free his wrists. This tightened the band around his Root and finally put him in such pain he had to stop. When she was sure he was helpless, Bahloul called in the palace guard, who were in

readiness without. They overpowered Shimshin and put
out his eyes.

His punishment was to be bound like a bull to the
grinding wheel at Timnath mill, and he ground our grain
for many days, while those who had been crippled or lost
family members to the man's random attacks came to
revile him. They spat and cursed and threw animal dung
over him. Children ran in under his feet to trip him up and
torment him with their whittled sticks. In response the
man would bellow in anger and pain. People began to call
him "the Bull".

If his own people were aware of his state, they made
no attempt to negotiate for his release at any time.

After a time even the most grieved lost interest in
him, and he might have been left at the grinding wheel
forever, had not the Baal Bull unexpectedly fallen ill and
died. It was a new young bull, and no other bull was
trained in the *Urda* ceremony. One of the Congress Priests
said, in jest, "We should bring in the Bull who grinds our
grain to mate with the white heifer."

All present laughed, but some were taken with the
idea, and it slowly gained force. And on the next *Urda* Day,
to his bewilderment, we did indeed bathe and perfume the
prisoner as if he were the sacred bull, even tying a wreath
of flowers round his neck. The *Urda* Priestess led him into
the Great Hall to much appreciation. He roared his
confusion, sounding more like a bull than ever, and our
delighted laughter surely reached the Great Above.

But then he heard the music and smelled the *murtu'u*
oil. He knew he was in the Congress Hall, and the Lady
gave him urgent desire. It lifted both his heads, and he

cried out his hunger. The *Urda* Priestess drew him on, and before he could be aware, he had embedded his Root not in her, but in the heifer. When he grasped the hairy rump and understood the trick that had been played on him it was too late. He could not resist his own urgency and sent up his pleasure cries with loud abandon. We cheered and applauded, but instead of accepting our approval he bellowed defiance at us.

After that the prisoner was taken off the grinding wheel, and lived in a hut in the temple enclosure, where we fed him well and bathed him in the purification pool. Every month he and the white heifer performed the rites, for although he always roared his distaste, he could not resist the opportunity for pleasure, and it seemed he even grew to appreciate our applause.

But the Congress Priestess Shilah, remembering the pleasure he had given her before and taking pity on him, bathed him and brought him into the hall one Lady Day to perform the rites with her. The pleasure of both of them was wonderful to behold.

Then other women also were drawn to worship with him. He never properly executed the poses and sequences, but his great strength and profound enjoyment seemed to excite the Lady herself. She was bountiful in the dispensation of pleasure for all, and Shimshin's Root needed only a touch to rise to readiness again.

But his god was stronger than we knew. During the New Year Festival, on Great Nammu Day, Shimshin brought disaster on us.

There was a very large group of celebrants, and even more witnesses. Shimshin was led in the *Char* Congress with a woman from Gaza, who, hearing of him, had come to celebrate at Timnath for the first time. When their ritual concluded to much approval, Shimshin asked her to lead him to the pillars of the temple. Thinking it part of our rites, she led him between the central supports of the balcony. There he was out of the view of the spectators above, and the worshippers were all engaged in ritual.

His strength was phenomenal, as was fully visible in that moment, for as he stood between the supports, he wrapped his hands around them and, calling on his god to give him strength, pulled them. The balcony shook so that those witnessing the rites above were alarmed. Their wild milling caused the balcony to sway and yaw. Shimshin cried out his triumph and pulled the harder.

The balcony pitched down into the midst of the celebrants in the Great Hall, most of whom had been slow to understand what was happening. Many were injured and thirty died, including Shimshin. The piteous cries of the wounded and dying surely reached the Great Above.

Shimshin's body we delivered to the nearest Elohist village.

THE TESTIMONY OF YA-MAR

Recorded by the Temple Scribe Indala on Fera Day of Allmother in Bunu Moon, in the fortieth year of the reign of Queen Imona, Priestess of Geshur.

I am Ya-Mar, daughter of Princess Maka of Geshur. My Allmother is Imona, Queen of Geshur, Priestess of the Lady. My mother's marriage with the Elohist King Daud was made to seal a peace treaty between Geshur and the Elohists, who were attacking the cities near Geshur, with great trouble to all.

I was born the second of four children, with one older brother, Absalom, and two younger, Bilgah and then Efrod, who died before he reached his tenth year.

We were raised in the Elohist belief, by the King's command. My mother tried to teach us in secret about the Great Lady, her hymns and wisdom. But I worshipped Elohi as instructed, and in those days I believed worship of Our Lady to be an evil.

When I was twelve my mother died giving birth to another daughter, who died with her. Absalom became our protector.

The king's other wives had many children. In the Elohist way we were called sisters and brothers, and we called the king father.

My true brother Absalom was older than me by five years. He was fierce and loving, protecting us if any of the others troubled us, and interceding for us at the palace. He was by far the most handsome of all the brothers, and was much loved by everyone. Even King Daud favoured Absalom, though Amnon, the eldest, was his named heir.

One day, approaching my fifteenth year, as I sat with my sisters in the courtyard sifting grain, I received a summons from the king commanding me to go to the house of Amnon, who was ill, and bake a Geshur delicacy for him. This honeybread, which my mother had taught me to make, was known to be healing for the sick.

I was uneasy for a reason I couldn't name, but when I hesitated, Amnon's true sisters berated me, and I had been taught to obey the king in all things. So I went to Amnon's house and prepared the honeybread for him. I set it on a tray for his servant to take to him.

But Amnon called out that I should bring it myself. The servant led me into the bedroom, and then Amnon ordered everyone else to go, and the men got up and took their leave. The servant, too, went out.

I knelt and set the tray on the floor near his pallet and pushed it towards him. But he said, "I am too weak. Bring it to me and feed me with your own hand."

I didn't know how to disobey. All my life I had been obedient to the king and those they called my brothers, as Elohi's law commands. I took up one of the little breads, knelt closer, and reached it to him.

He did not eat the bread. He was not ill. He reared up, grabbed my wrist, and pulled me down beside him, saying, "Lie with me, sister. It is not honeybread that I need from Geshur. You've been slanting your eyes at me for months past. Let us serve the Lady together."

I cried, "My brother, this is not the way with us. I have not been consecrated to the Lady, but to Elohi. You know I am a virgin. If you use me in this way shame will cover me for all my life. I can never face our people again. Please let me go."

His face was closed and red, and when I saw how determined he was, I began to struggle, and screamed for help. Some must have heard me, but none came.

Amnon was a big man, and strong. He hurt me with the worst pain I have ever felt. I wept and pleaded for him to stop, but he went on till he was sated. Then he rolled off my body onto his back, put his arm up over his eyes and said, "You disgust me, woman. Get out of my house."

I pleaded with him, desperate not to face anyone in this humiliation. I reminded him that by Elohist law he should marry me to lift my shame. But his servant came at his command and pushed me out of the house just as I was—hair and scarves and robe askew, clutching myself in pain, my blood on my thighs. They locked the door against me.

I fell down, screaming and tearing my hair, and fainted. When I awoke, they had carried me to the palace.

Absalom my true brother heard and came at once. I told him I could not live another hour. The shame would attach to me forever. I begged him to help me.

But Absalom swore he would avenge me. He promised the shame would be lifted. He told me that the shame was not mine, but Amnon's, as my mother's people decreed. He pleaded with me only to wait, and took me to live in his own house. I did not go outside the house for two years, so dark was the grief that afflicted me.

One day Absalom came to me and said, "All the brothers are coming to dine with us. Do not enter the hall, but go and stand in the serving passage and watch at the peephole."

I cried, "Do you ask me to look upon the face of Amnon?"

"For one hour only," he said. "Be strong, like our mother." So I watched as the brothers came in and sat down around the spread cloth laden with food. Amnon was guided by a servant to a place close to where I was hidden, so that I saw only his back.

They ate and drank as I watched. A servant with a winejar stayed close to Amnon, keeping his cup filled over a long hour. Then Amnon told a story about one of his rams, laughing too loudly. He reeled back drunkenly on his cushion, and I saw that same red, swollen face I had seen while he raped me. The sight blinded me. I heard Absalom cry aloud, "Today I remember my sister Tamar," and could see again.

At his words three servants ran in with naked knives. Two held Amnon's arms, stabbing his chest and abdomen, while the third pulled back his head and slit his throat. Blood fountained up for a moment, and then I saw no more, for all the others, fearing for their own lives, leapt to their feet, shouting and calling for their servants as they ran from the house. Soon came the sound of hooves.

Absalom was left alone. He came and put a knife into my hand, then led me to where Amnon lay dying. He drew back the torn and bloody robe. I saw his root again.

"Those who worship the Lady, as our mother did, have a law for such as Amnon. You are the Priestess now," Absalom said. "Do what is right."

For a moment I recoiled in horror. Then I heard my mother speak in my heart, reciting from the Wisdom, as she had on a day when we learned that one of the sisters was to marry a man who had raped her. *Among us, his Root would be taken by the Castration Priestess! Scripture says, "She will not offer it to the Lady but throw it for the dogs to devour."*

And then rage came to me—from the Lady or my mother, I did not know, and I lifted the knife. Amnon's eyes opened and he stared at me. I cut off his root with two hacking strokes as he died, and held the vile flesh up. Absalom led me to the outer door, whistling up the dogs, and I threw it to them. They squabbled over it, biting and tearing at it and each other.

And for the first time I recited aloud a verse from the Scriptures, one that my mother had repeated to us many times. *"The Allmother is All. She is birth and death. She is the Great Above and the Great Below."* That day I felt its truth and its holiness.

Absalom said, "They will come for me. We must go to our family in Geshur. Gather only what you need for travel and come at once."

Absalom came with a horse and I mounted behind him. Dawn was just breaking. We travelled very fast.

In Geshur I was given sanctuary for a time in the Lady's temple, where the Priestesses and my Allmother attended to me. They put ointments in my Vulva to draw out the pain that still troubled me, and made spells to draw the horror from my spirit. They changed my name for the Goddess, and I became Ya-Mar.

I went to live in my Allmother's palace. There I studied the things my mother had tried to teach me, repenting the blind stubbornness that had prevented me from seeing the truth when she spoke it.

Absalom my brother was summoned and has now returned to the king. Before he left, he promised to punish the king, too, for what had been done to me. But I will never return among the Elohists even when Absalom is king.

Now I have at last been accepted into kinship with the Lady. On my Consecration Day they led the Pleasure Priestess in to me for the first time. Denarsh was not at all like Amnon, in appearance or in manner. She was beautiful, patient, and knowing, and when for the first time I sent the love offering to the Great Mother, I truly felt Her presence and Her blessing, and I wept in gratitude.

THE TESTIMONY OF ARNOAN

This is the testimony of Arnoan, daughter of Afula, as told to the Scribe-Historian Priestess Indala, and attested by the High Priestess of the temple of Dimnod on Lat Day in Daughter week of Ashur Moon, in the 8th year of the reign of Queen Boudahl

A t the time I was sent my first sacred Vulva Blood, my father was overseer of all the olive groves of Kereth-Baal, an Elohist who had just inherited the orchards from his father, as is the custom among the Elohists.

One morning in Naruju Moon, shortly before I was to be taken into kindredship with the Lady, Kereth-Baal came to the orchard at Tigla where my father and our people were gathering olives. I had come to them as usual at midday, and was spreading a cloth for their lunch. Kereth-Baal stopped his mule by my cloth and gazed at me with a look of congress hunger. I had seen him many times before, and admired him, for he sometimes worshipped at our hill shrine, and was a fine man to whom the Lady had been generous. But this was the first time he had looked at me so.

He said, "Your breasts are a woman's breasts now, Arnoan." His eyes glowed with admiration, his hair was thick and curling, his thighs were strong, and his Goddess Root bulged against the mule's neck.

I proudly parted the panels of my over-robe to his better view and said, "I will make the Third Consecration next Moon." He asked me for food, and I gave him cheese and bread and olives. He ate watching me as I spread the meal for the workers.

The next day early, Kereth-Baal returned to the orchard and called my father into his tent. There he offered my father a golden Lady icon in Her form as a heifer and said that he would give the orchard at Tigla into my father's ownership if I would accept him as consort. My father came home and reported this to my mother and me.

My mother Afula warned me earnestly not to accept an Elohist. "Their god is a God of Death, he hates our Great Lady of Life the Queen of Heaven," she said. "He is well called jealous because he wants Her power and shares nothing. Our Lady does not count him among Her sons. She has repudiated him as consort, and so should you, any man who worships him."

But I admired Kereth-Baal. I remembered the look in his eyes, and the way his Tree had swelled as he gazed at me.

I knew, too, that my father wanted me to have the orchard, for it was one of those that had belonged to his Allmother[12] before the Elohists came. The invaders killed many of her workers and took possession of her orchards and vineyards, and Elohists have them to this day.

I thought that if we married, Kereth-Baal's orchards and vineyards would naturally belong to his wife and her daughters. My mother warned me that no Elohist man would observe the Lady's Law in property whomever he married, but I thought of the look in his eyes, and imagined I was doing the Lady's will.

So I was allowed to send my approval to Kereth-Baal, and accepted his further gifts of oil, wine, grain and worship tokens, and my mother agreed that as soon as I had entered into kindredship with the Lady, she would order the marriage celebrations.

But seven days later, when I was on my way to the olive grove again with food for my father and the workers, Kereth-Baal came down upon me with several men and a priest of their temple and dragged me into a close stand of trees. There was a small Lady shrine, but they ignored it.

The priest began to recite and make signs over us, then said to me, "You are Kereth-Baal's wife in the eyes of Elohi and must go with him to his house. You will cover your breasts and your hair and be obedient to your husband, for he is your master and you are under his command."

In my indignation I cried that I could not take any consort until I had performed my first-fruits offering at the temple. I said that no man could be master of a wife, that it was for men to serve their wives and that Kereth-Baal had agreed that it was so.

The priest was at first shocked, as if he had never been spoken to so before. Then he was angry. He said that no follower of Elohi could marry a *harlot* who had been *wanton* at a temple of *perversion*, and that my first-fruit offering belonged not to the Goddess but to my husband. The words he used I did not then understand.

Kereth-Baal made to put me on a mule. But I broke free, and I was small and nimble and outran them all among the trees.

Had my mother learned about this, she would not have let the marriage go forward, but I told no one. And when Kereth-Baal sent another gift, a jewelled bracelet, only I knew that it was an atonement. I accepted the gift, believing that it signalled repentance in him.

When the time came, my mother arranged my celebration for the third Lady Day of Upara and led me to the temple with the High Priestess and the Priestesses in attendance. There I performed the sacred rite with Her Pleasure Priest, who saw that the Lady was well pleased with me. I remained with him a night and a day while he taught me those holy pleasures as are named among her best gifts to her people, and I learned well.

On Lady Day of Daughter Week of Timun, my mother summoned Kereth-Baal, and my marriage was performed. My consort seemed happy and lighthearted and declared that he would sacrifice at the hill-shrine to show his gratitude to the Lady. His Goddess Root was strong and eager, and the Lady was well pleased with our worship.

If we had stayed to live in my mother's house, as is the way of our people, it would perhaps have been well. But among the strange customs of his people the strangest is this: daughters go to live with their consort's mother, the sons bring their wives to their mother's house.

With us it is the opposite, for how can a woman leave her mother? But a man must cleave to his wife. That is the Lady's wisdom, and who can deny that it is best? Again my mother advised me not to agree, to insist on my right to remain with her. But I was curious about his strange god and his mother was at first very kind.

For three months, my Vulva Blood came as usual on Lat Day. But in Daughter Week of Bunu, I knew the Goddess would bless me with a daughter, and I made sure that my consort watered my womb well that night and the nights following.

Early in Mother Week Kereth-Baal told me he would make his usual visit to all his vineyards and orchards. He was to be away many weeks.

I objected strongly to this. I reminded him that it was a law among my people and his own that when a woman marries, she and her consort stay close, renouncing all other cares and obligations, for one year; that we do not even perform congress worship with others during that year. I said it was wrong for us to be apart.

But he was determined. I told him that I would go to my mother until his return.

On Lat Day my Vulva-Blood did not come, and I regretted even more that Kereth-Baal had gone. But I had no way to send to him.

I remained with my mother through the moons of Char, Atana and Utana, Turm, and Ashur. In Allmother Week of Ashur Moon, the child quickened in me. I went to the hill shrine and spoke to the daughter of my womb to learn her name.

I went back to his mother's house when Kereth-Baal returned at the end of Ashur Moon. On the evening of our return, I invited Kereth-Baal to my room, prepared the celebration, and dressed in purple linen. When he came and sat with me, I offered him the cup, told him of my daughter, and spoke her name. I invited him to call her name and drink from the cup.

Kereth-Baal did not take the cup. He frowned at the floor and asked, "Whose seed is the child? Does it belong to that temple whore?"

So deep was I in my joy that I hardly heard, then. I said, "I felt the Lady send her blessing in Bunu Moon. I was sure then that it would come to pass."

I offered him the cup again, but it fell from his hand, and the elixir I had made splattered over the floor. I was distressed at this omen, but Kereth-Baal comforted me and said that he was very tired but that we would celebrate the ritual another day.

On the following day he came to me saying, "My beloved wife, come with me to my own temple, that I may give thanks to my lord for this blessing and make the child's name known to my priest. I will take an offering of barley meal."

I helped him measure the barley—in the prescribed amount, he told me, for a thank offering. So jealous is their god that he measures offerings to the smallest grain.

We went into the temple. When the priest came out to greet us Kereth-Baal took my hand, led me towards the altar, and told me to set down the grain offering.

It was the priest who had called the marriage rites while they held me prisoner months before. I began then to fear that Kereth-Baal meant treachery, but how? He held me hard by the wrist and I knew he would rather break my bones than let me go.

The priest smiled and lifted a scroll. "Your husband tells me that you are pregnant," he said. "Is it so?"

I said, "It is certain. My daughter has moved within me and told me her name."

"But the child is not your husband's seed, but that of the temple whore to whom you gave the virginity which rightly belonged to your husband?"

I said, "Do not take the sacred words of my language and twist them into something your god despises. The child is the Lady's seed, how could it be otherwise? My husband watered the seed during Daughter Week in the Moon of Bunu."

"Your husband believes that you have been unfaithful to him."

"Unfaithful?" I cried. "My faith is pledged to the Lady Yahu and I am ever faithful!"

The priest said to Kereth-Baal, "Stop her mouth." My consort pressed his hand over my face so that I choked.

And then I understood them, and fear and regret filled me. For a man who will stop the mouth of a woman in such a way has so closed his ears to Goddess wisdom that he is dead. Who has ever known such a thing? And for a priest to command such in the name of their god and for a man to obey such a command—then I knew that they were all insane, god, priest, and consort together. I struggled, but Kereth-Baal held me fast, one hand over my mouth pressing my head back against his chest, the other twisting my arm behind his back so harshly that my shoulder tore.

Outrage flamed in me so hot my consort was burned, for I sensed him shrink. But he was under the control of his priest. The priest looked at me with sly triumph in his eyes, like the wolf that I chased out of my mother's fowlhouse one morning, a goose broken in its mouth.

He said, "If you have let yourself be defiled, you must suffer the punishment. If you are not defiled, you have nothing to fear. If your husband's suspicions are false, you will bear the child."

In a panic, though I didn't know what to fear, I tried to tear Kereth-Baal's hand from my face, but he is a large man and held me hard.

The priest set down a cup and flask on the table, then picked up a scroll and opened it.

"This is our scripture, the word of the one god Elohi," he said to me. "It has a message for you. Listen, wanton whore, and understand the truth and the law."

He began to read from the scroll. Their god speaks a formal language that is difficult, but he read with such slow pomposity that I understood.

"If no man have lain with thee, and if thou hast not gone aside to uncleanness with another instead of thy husband, and if thou be not defiled, be thou free from this bitter water that causeth the curse.

"But if thou hast gone aside to another instead of thy husband, and if thou be defiled, and some man have lain with thee beside thine husband, then may you be a curse and a shame among thy people, when Elohi doth make thy thigh to rot, and thy belly to swell."

The priest set the scroll on the table. He picked up the flask and poured liquid into the cup, saying,

"And this water that causeth the curse shall go into thy bowels, to make thy belly to swell, and thy thigh to rot.

"I have read the curse to her," he said. "Keep hold on her mouth. As she is an unbeliever, let it be as if she has said, *So be it.*" He stooped and with one hand he drew some dust from the floor. Then through Kereth-Baal's suffocating hand the scent of the liquid suddenly came to me.

It was the Lat Day herb.

As the priest shook the dust into the cup, I bit my consort's hand and he let go. I cried, "My daughter has moved in me, and I have heard her name. I cannot drink this herb, it will cause me to miscarry."

They pretended not to hear. Kereth-Baal let go my arm to take up the bowl of barley, but I knocked it down. The priest bent and scooped the grains back into the bowl, murmuring his foul curses.

"Let it be as if I took it from her hand," he said.

A moment later the choking smoke of burning grain rose up from his altar fire. But it was the smell of the Lat Day herb that made my throat sicken.

"Hold her," the priest ordered.

Kereth-Baal dragged my mouth open. Between them they forced me to swallow the poisoned water in the cup.

"Elohi ordains that the water shall enter her body," the priest said. They laid me on the table and opened my skirts, and then the priest thrust an empty reed into my Vulva, hard up against my womb. I felt my daughter move in anxious understanding, but how could I reassure her?

He took a mouthful of the foul liquid, crouched down, put his mouth to the reed, and blew the poison into my Vulva. When he pulled the reed out, there was blood. My stomach heaved and I cried out.

Then Kereth-Baal lifted his hands from me and let me stand. I screamed at them for the evil they had done. My consort hung his head, but the priest only lifted the scroll again and read:

"Then shall the man be guiltless from iniquity, and the woman shall bear her iniquity."

I said, "This foul god you worship, may the Lady turn his curses back on you from now until the end of the world."

I went back to the house and gathered all my posses-
sions and the holy icons, for I would not leave anything
sacred to the Lady in that polluted place. My consort
followed me to the barn, afraid to touch me without his
priest to give him courage. I mounted my mule and turned
its head towards the road.

Kereth-Baal said, "You may have other children,
Arnoan, but they must be my seed."

I spat in his face all the snot and blood and tears that
had collected in my mouth and returned to the house of
my mother, which I should never have left. I lost my
daughter four days afterwards. Her name was Mashouka.

PETITION FROM THE TEMPLE AT URUS

From High Priestess Inayah of Urus and Tomen, daughter of Marbunta, to the Most Holy the High Priestess Oloaya of Yarosaleem. Recorded by the Priestess-Scribe Atabeh on Lat Day of Allmother Week of Turm in the 12th year of the reign of Oloaya, High Priestess of Yarosaleem

The Elohists are fighting among themselves again, this time in the fields around Urus. It is very troubling to our people in the area, as there are groups of armed men roaming the countryside. They steal livestock and raid gardens, threatening and even killing anyone who protests. Their battles take place wherever the opposing groups happen to meet. It is dangerous for anyone caught between them.

It has not been easy to get information about what has caused this, but one of our spies has sent a report. The problem arises in the Elohist belief that Elohi forbids men to join in congress worship together. Some among them apparently insist that it is acceptable so long as the men are strangers to each other, or from different tribes.

In towns near to our temples, things are easy for men who prefer to worship with men, because our Congress Priests are considered "strangers", even after multiple visits. In small villages that are entirely the Elohists' own, however, this causes hardship, because the inhabitants are likely to be all of one tribe. As a result, whenever a stranger passes through such a town, desperate men may demand congress from him.

Our spy thinks that a couple stopped overnight in an Elohist village near Urus, and a group of men invited the husband to congress worship. He rejected the invitation as an insult to Elohi. When they persisted, this man pushed his young wife out of the house and told them to sate themselves with her, locking the door against her. The men tortured and raped her on the doorstep while she screamed and pleaded for help from within. They did not let up until, early in the morning, she died. According to our spy, she had been defiled in every possible way.

The woman's consort then called upon his tribe to punish the tribe of the men involved. According to Elohist law, the husband is guilty of nothing, all blame falls on the violators. So his tribe has willingly come to his aid, and the tribe of the violators is forced to respond.

The fighting has been raging around Urus for weeks. Our people cannot work their fields or tend their livestock, for fear of coming across blood-crazed Elohists or finding their pasture a battle zone and their sheep panicked if not killed. It is useless to protest to their leaders: when they are bent on their god's work, they despise measure and reason. In any case, every roving band has its own commander, and they do not seem to be responsible to any higher authority. The only solution seems to be to let this blood madness wear itself out.

We therefore sue to be allowed to open the storage warehouse and dispense grains, smoked meat, and vegetables in the usual measure to those who cannot access their gardens or livestock, and animal feed for those whose herds are prevented from foraging.

The Testimony of Eanna

This is the history of the birth of my son who is now the Elohist High Priest, with the reason he was given to the Elohist temple. Recorded by the Priestess-Scribe Indala in the presence of the High Priestess Orla in the 5th year of her reign.

W hen I was a young girl not yet consecrated to Our Lady, it was the habit of my friends and me to gather at the village spring every morning where we drew water, the first of our household tasks. One bright morning as we stood chatting and laughing together a little longer than usual, a strange rider stopped and asked us to pour some water for his horse.

The others were all too surprised to obey, for not only was a horse an unusual sight in our poor village, but the man—as we could see from his leg bindings and the way he dressed his hair—was an Elohist. Elohists often worshipped at our hill shrine on high festival days, but they rarely appeared in the village, and I had never seen this man before.

But I had just drawn a bucket of water, and half nerves, half bravado, I poured it into the stone bowl that farmers used for their donkeys. The horse was thirsty and pushed its head against me as I poured, so that I dropped my bucket. It fell against the bowl with a loud crash, the horse tossed up its head, and I shrieked and stumbled. The Elohist caught my arm to steady me.

My friends picked up their own buckets and scattered. The Elohist dismounted and I drew another bucket of water for his horse, then one for myself. All the while he stared at me blinking, like a man coming awake after a heavy sleep.

"My name is Elkanah, of Ramah," he said. And then, "Who is your father?"

The question was very strange to me. I said, "My mother is Ushera. My name is Eanna." Then I took my bucket and went as fast I could home.

Two days later the stranger came to our house with gifts asking to marry me. He was a rich man and his gifts of oil and wine and barley seemed munificent to us. When my mother protested that I had not yet been consecrated and therefore couldn't marry, the stranger said that as his wife he would ask me to leave off the worship of the Lady and instead worship Elohi with him and his family. I could visit Her temple, if I insisted, but I was never to take part in consecration or congress worship.

He said Elohists believed it was wrong for a woman to have congress worship with anyone other than her husband, but I didn't understand the reason he gave, which made my mother snort in derision.

He said I would have clothes of dyed Egyptian linen and gold earrings and my own donkey. He promised my father regular supplies of honey, barley, and oil if he would let me go. I remember my father looking at my mother with a worried frown, and the way his fingers rubbed the spot between his eyebrows as if by that means he could push away the question itself.

My mother said it was not possible and asked him to take back his gifts, but he would not take them, and when he left we were glad to have them, for there was hardship among us. We had already lost two lambs to sickness that season and feared there would be more. As for me, I was entranced with the promise of fine linen and gold and the thought of plenty for my family.

He came three more times, always with gifts, and I pleaded to be allowed to marry him. My mother was unhappy and told me I didn't understand what I was sacrificing, but at last agreed. So when the time of the Third Consecration came, I went not to our temple, but to live with my husband Elkanah in Ramah.

I did not send pleasure to the Allmother's dreams on our wedding night. When Elkanah had satisfied himself, which was very soon, he leapt up and went to announce it to the guests in the great room while I still lay in bed. His mother and sisters came in and pushed me aside to snatch up the linen sheet and examine it for the blood gift which rightly belonged to the Lady. They took the sheet to the crowd without, and I heard cheers and congratulations. When the women returned my husband stayed to carouse with his friends.

I was confused. I said, "When will my husband return to pleasure me for the Allmother?" They only scolded and told me that a woman's pleasure in congress was a trick of the Evil One. They began performing rites to 'purify' me. I said to them, "The rite of congress is holiness itself. It pleases the Allmother, what is this?"

Then they spat and said the Allmother was a disguise of the Evil One and I must not even mention Her name for fear of the wrath of Elohi. I shouted to them to bring my husband back to me. Instead, they left me, with warnings about how I should avert my eyes and bend my head down when speaking to my husband, and always to wait for him to speak to me first. And I was never to expect pleasure from our congress, they repeated. Elohi designed congress for the pleasure of men, and it was the Evil One who tempted women to pleasure, which it was every woman's duty to resist.

I told them what they said was blasphemy.

I was too distressed to pleasure myself, and I knew that that could not satisfy the Lady on a wedding night. When my husband returned to me much later, he did not understand my indignation, and took refuge in believing that I missed my mother—the fate, he said, of all new brides. I told him that the Lady required the pleasure offering from me as well as from him, that it was a part of duty, and that what he had done was an insult to Her.

He was very surprised, but said that he loved me and he would try. His Tree was alive again, but his imagination went no further than the *upara* posture, and I stopped him and invited him to the Kissing of the Goddess Flower.

Elkanah drew back from me with a look of distaste. He said, "That is unclean! How can I set my mouth to what is despised by Elohi?"

This shocked me into silence, and I stared at him in such outrage his gaze fell. He muttered, "It is forbidden."

I felt the Lady's rage. I said, "The Holy Vulva of the Lady is sacred, as is the reflection of it in all Her daughters. Elohi was cast out by the Lady Yahu for his cruelties and was not allowed to worship with Her again. That is why he forbids these pleasures to you."

His eyes still avoided mine. He said, "You promised to learn Elohi worship."

I said, "How could I guess that it would mean such blasphemy against the Great Lady?"

Then the Lady withdrew the gift of desire from him, and his Root could not be raised again that night.

I knew She was displeased with me and I was sick with regret for what I had done. But there was hardship among my family, for around our village that season there was olive blight and too much rain, so that crops rotted in the fields. And Elkanah was generous with gifts to them, and I grew fond of him.

I learned to worship Elohi with strange rituals and taboos: they considered Vulva blood unclean and did not make medicines with it; there was no congress worship in the temple; and they didn't stand naked in Elohi's eyes the way we do for the Lady.

Elkanah said that all such sacred rites were evil in Elohi's eyes, who only loves blood sacrifice. I asked why he worshipped such a cruel god, but he could only say that it was what his people did.

Elkanah did not know any of the congress postures apart from *upara*, and because I had not been for my Consecration, I did not know how to instruct him. I tried to tell him what I had witnessed on festival days when Asherah and Dumuzzi perform the sacred rituals in the holy sanctuary[13], but he would not hear me, saying such things were forbidden. My mother had given me the bride gift that is traditional among us, but he disdained to use any of the pleasure baubles or ointments it contained.

I had little joy in our congress. Elkanah said he loved me and came to me often, and sometimes the Lady did send promising heat to my Vulva. But our efforts did not succeed, and never did I sweeten the Allmother's dreams in our congress. This failure weighed on my spirit.

In obedience to the Lady's law, I would not have gone to engage in temple worship that year, even if I had been willing to break my promise to Elkanah. But the women of the household watched me closely, convinced that I would—not least Elkanah's other wife, Nina.

She was pregnant when I arrived in the household, with her third child. She often said she hoped for a boy. I asked why, since she had one son already. I learned that Elohists believe that a man's Root carries a seed that is planted in a woman and that becomes a child. A man prizes a wife who births sons, they said, because a son will carry the same seed in his Root and so pass it into other women. Among them a woman who has many sons is highly valued.

I laughed when they told me this. I asked why then no Congress Priest, nor any other man, ever bore a child? And how could a seed be taken from a man's Root and put into that of a new-born boy, a where did the seed go when a girl was born? But no such reasoning made them think.

Nina gave birth to a boy and went about solemnly praising the benevolence of Elohi. I knew this was simply to spite and mock me. So I laughed and repeated that none but the Lady blessed the womb, that it is She who places the child there, not any male, god or human. I said that the real blessing was a daughter, who would be a mother in her turn.

I yearned for a daughter, but whatever I yearned for, I was destined for grief, because the Lady never blessed me. I could not wonder at that. I knew that until I sent the pleasure offering to the Allmother's dreams, I could not hope for the blessing of a child.

The women sneered and asked me why, if the Lady was so bountiful, she had not blessed my womb. I told them I would visit the temple of Asherah and beg her for a daughter and then we would see. But they accused me of wanting to visit the temple to worship with a stranger, and would not let me have oil for an offering.

I purchased a small jar and secreted it in the pantry, and each day was able to draw a little oil off from the table jar, which Elkanah's mother replenished daily from the stores.

And after Nina gave birth, I escaped the vigilance of the women and made my way to the temple with my small hoard of oil. There the Prophecy Priestess looked at me with black, burning eyes and said, "You come with scant oil and veiled breasts and yet seek the favour of the Lady. How can her blessing enter a womb that sends no pleasure service to the Allmother?"

I was so shocked at this knowing I could hardly open my mouth. Then I said, "My husband is an Elohist not versed in the ways of pleasure."

She replied, "If your husband will not learn the ways, you must go to seek the favour of the one he worships, he who was cast out by Yahu and cursed to come between the Allmother and Her people till the day they awaken and turn back to Her. Seek Elohi's aid, since that is the path and the people you have chosen. If you have a son, you will give him to Elohi, since he values only the male, but if you have a daughter, you may bring her as a remorse offering to the Lady, to be raised in the holiness which you in your foolishness have abandoned."

I returned to my husband's home broken in spirit, and the instruction weighed on my heart for many moons.

In Setaru Moon Elkanah made preparations to go up to an important shrine in Shiloh, to make a sacrifice. At his request I went with him. We arrived early in the afternoon, and Elkanah left me at the temple gate while he went to join a crowd of men waiting to buy sacrifice animals.

The Shiloh temple was not at all like their temple in Ramah. It was big and imposing, with golden doors and marble facing and great golden horns above. I was in awe, for although I had heard of such splendour, I had never seen anything so beautiful, and I thought that this god must have power. I began at once to plead with Elohi. I hardly knew how to address him directly, and it felt strange and uncomfortable to make my appeal to anyone but the Lady. I feared I would surely offend Her, even though Her priestess had instructed me. I couldn't catch my breath.

An old man was sitting there by the entrance, and he knew me for a stranger and began to berate me for impiety. But I said, "No, old man, you mistake. My husband is an Elohist as are you, and I have left the Lady to worship Elohi. Now I plead with Elohi for the child I crave. If he gives me a son, I will dedicate the boy to this temple—and that is what I have been saying to your lord."

The old man said, "Go inside and speak to Phineas, my son, the priest of Elohi. Let him hear your prayer, for its passage to Elohi is more certain that way."

Elkanah had not returned.

I gathered my courage and followed a man and woman and their squealing lambs into the temple court. Inside a huge courtyard people stood waiting with their sacrifice animals while attendants—as in the Ramah temple, every one male—spoke to them. There was not a single priestess.

A broad gate in the far wall led to an inner space where I could see men going up and down a staircase, tending the altar fire above.

Even with such brilliance, I did not see any tapestry on the walls. Our poor village shrine had a most beautiful tapestry of the Lady in sacred *Naruju* congress with her consort, which my mother had helped to stitch as a young girl. And in the great temple in Tyre, I knew, there were thirteen, one for each of the Sacred Postures, and gold statues of the Lady. I was amazed that such a magnificent temple had none.

There were three doors in the wall beside me, of polished bronze. They glowed like fire. As I gazed about me, nervous and undecided, the door nearest me opened, and a man came out. He wore a robe of fine linen, gold rings and necklaces, and a jewelled headdress, like a High Priestess.

He looked at me, frowning in surprise. I said quickly, "I seek the priest Phineas."

"I am Phineas," he said. "What is it you wish?" His manner and voice so frightened me I could only stare at him. "You may speak," he said.

Then I told him my trouble—that I wanted a child and that the Lady had turned Her face away from my pleading because I had not sent Her the pleasure offering, and that I had been instructed to seek Elohi's favour.

He paused for a moment, gazing hard at me, then gestured and led me back into the inner room. There the ceiling was draped with fine blue and purple cloth. A long table held candlesticks and scrolls. The seat-cushions that lined the walls were tasselled in gold and silver. There were gold and silver trays on stands of carved cedar. I had never seen anywhere so resplendent. I was awestruck.

He closed the door. "How comes it that you were not consecrated in your own temple when your time came?" he asked.

"My husband conditioned for that when we married."

"Who is your husband?" he enquired, but he seemed to know. "Elkanah?" I nodded.

"He is making an offering today."

"And you will make your own." He bent and lifted a golden cloth from the cushions to reveal soft white linen. "Take off your mantle and sit down," he said, and he was so strange and impressive that I had no thought but to obey.

"I am familiar with the Lady's rites," he said.

He lifted his jewelled headdress and set it on the table, then took off his own mantle and lifted his robe. His Goddess Root was as fine and strong as any I had seen in the temple on festival days.

He knelt before me and lifted my underdress to reveal my Vulva. He smiled, drew my knees apart, and exclaimed approvingly, "Ah, already the flower stamen stands proud!" He offered a worship kiss.

I babbled, "Is it not forbidden by Elohi?"

"It is forbidden to all but a few. The secret rites of Elohi are allowed only to us. Those who are chosen may not speak of it to anyone. This includes your husband. Do you promise this by the Lady's Vulva?"

I promised. I knew the Lady approved, for She was sending great pleasure heat into my Vulva. I recited the congress prayer and the priest said Amen. He took the *bao'u* posture and began the Kissing of the Honey Flower. I moved into the *ortha* posture at once. I sent many pleasure cries to the Allmother's ears even before we came to *Arba*, and then for the first time I sent the full pleasure offering to the Lady as was my duty, and when the pleasure softened, I wept for joy.

Phineas helped me to a basin of water where I bathed, then put on my mantle again. He said, "When you get home, be sure that your husband waters your womb again."

When I came out of the temple, Elkanah was leading a fine young lamb from the pens and many more worshippers were arriving. As I went to meet him, he looked at me and said, "How beautiful you are, my beloved wife! And what joy I feel to see you smile so!"

Even Nina saw the change, for when we returned to Ramah, she frowned at me and said, "Look how the barren wife smiles! Have you given her a priest-sized portion of the sacrifice again, Elkanah? For she has surely no other reason to smile."

That night I invited Elkanah to visit me, and as usual he took his pleasure quickly, but I thought of the pleasure Phineas had given me and was able to send a small thank-offering to the Lady. When my Vulva Blood did not come on Lat Day, I said, "If it is a boy, I will give him to Elohi." Elkanah agreed. I did not tell him that I had been instructed in this by the High Priestess. When my son was born, I named him for Elohi, not the Lady, and in his third year, after weaning him, I carried him to the temple at Shiloh.

There I met Phineas again, and again we performed the secret rites to his god, though in my heart I dedicated my own pleasure to the Lady. And she did approve it, for again she gifted me with a child, and indeed after three of our visits to Shiloh I was so gifted. I knew it was not Elohi's doing, though I allowed Elkanah and his family to believe so, for it was the Lady I held in my heart during these holy rites, and I sent my offering to Her.

After this, I sometimes found I could send pleasure when in congress with my husband, for he was concerned for my happiness and grew less anxious for his own pleasure.

Shemeloh my son grew into a fine child and was much approved by all who visited the Shiloh temple. I visited him every year at the time of sacrifice, always taking him gifts, and he was a loving child to me.

When he was ten years old there was war and we had word that the priest Phineas was killed. I mourned, for his kindness to me had been great.

Then my husband Elkanah, who had lost a number of his field hands to the army, had an accident working in the fields: he fell, and his head struck the plough. They carried him home and put him to bed. I immediately sent to my mother, for I knew that if he died I and my children would have little protection in his household, and the priest I might have appealed to was gone. Elkanah died within the month. My brother came to escort us back to my mother's house.

From that moment I never saw my son again, but we heard news of him, for Shemeloh grew in renown and is so respected by the Elohists that they consider him a holy man and appeal to him for judgement from all over the land. Blessings upon him there among his people, but I returned to the bosom of the Lady.

She allowed me to be consecrated, and even to serve as Congress Priestess in the temple at Yizreel, which was the greatest joy to me. She has blessed me with many children, altogether five daughters and three sons, excluding the one I gave to Elohi. They have all been raised in Her worship and were consecrated to Her in due course. She accepted one daughter from me, who is now High Priestess in the temple at Goddess Well.

I am forever grateful to the Lady for her bounty and forgiveness.

Recopied by the Scribe-Historian Dorin in the twelfth year of the reign of Lady Asmun

THE LETTERS OF YAHZEBUL

LETTER 1

To the most holy Ishnat, Queen of Tyre and Sidon, High Priestess of the Holy Shrines, Beloved of the Lady Asherah, daughter of Banab, High Priestess and Queen of Tyre and Sidon, descended through four hundred and five generations from Asherah, Daughter of the Great Goddess Yahu, from her loving and obedient daughter Yahzebul.

Beloved Mother, my best greetings,
My journey was completed on the eve of Lady Day. As we neared Ahab's city, we were slowed along the route by the crowds of people who came to welcome us. How happy they were! And as the great golden image of Our Lady Asherah passed, they held up their hands in Open Vulva, awestruck and reverent, as if receiving blessings from the very sight.

How they marvelled, too, at the long train of rich gifts that, through your generosity, accompanied your daughter! The shouting and cheering as we passed must have awakened the Great Above. The temple here, I find, has nothing to compare. The temple worthy to house Her that my consort Ahab has sworn to build is greatly needed, and when he announced this promise to the people, they were wild in their joy.

The priests of Elohi are very unhappy, just as you foretold. They are jealous and angry, like their god. On the day of our Consecration, several stood by the temple gates uttering ugly prophecies as we entered to perform the sacred rites, though they did not dare to prevent any from entering.

The ceremony was a source of great happiness to the people. They were hungry to have the kingship of Ahab authorized by the Lady, and when my consort knelt and I crowned him in Her name, the cheering deafened us.

Our worship ritual was joined by vast numbers, including very many whose dress showed them to be Elohists, for who can fail to love our benevolent Lady? My consort has a fine upstanding Root, as you promised me, and his people cried their admiration aloud. My Holy Vulva thrilled them even more, and when we took the *atana and utana* posture the pleasure we sent up was such as must fill Great Nammu's dreaming for a Moon.

LETTER 2

To the most holy Ishnat, Queen of Tyre and Sidon, High Priestess of the Holy Shrines, Beloved of the Lady Asherah, daughter of Banab, High Priestess and Queen of Tyre and Sidon, descended through four hundred and five generations from Asherah, Daughter of the Great Goddess Yahu, from her loving and obedient daughter Yahzebul, High Priestess and Queen of Israel.

My dear Mother,

The Elohists are a very strange group. They do not make any love offerings in their temple, and they condemn our own pleasure rites. Pleasure worship angers Elohi, they say, and causes him to punish them with failed crops and other disasters. How can one explain the willing worship of this cruel god?

No women serve in the temple; women are forbidden even to step into the Holy Sanctuary there. When I heard this, I asked why the priests performed the pleasure rites only among themselves? They responded with horror. Men, including priests, must even cover their Roots in the temple, and women hide their Holy Vulvas: Elohi takes no joy in the sight. No one can explain why.

Their offerings—and many are required of them—are not merely of grain, field fruits, oil, and animals, but also of linen, gold, and precious stones. Strangest of all, the temple has no larders for the storage of oils and grains, no smoke rooms. All the offerings become the property, not of the temple, but of the priests, according to their rank. When I asked a priest how they feed their people in times of famine, he opened his mouth and stared at me before saying, "Elohi demands greater offerings at such times, so that his priests may thrive."

The priests are very rich. They go about draped in fine clothing and gold, and the children consecrated to the temple walk before them in the streets, sweeping the path or waving fans. Four temple children carry a canopy of purple linen for the Chief Priest, and the people step out of his way as he passes.

And it is not enough for them that they worship this god themselves: they repeatedly urge my consort to swear loyalty to Elohi and send soldiers to demolish our shrines. Work has begun on the Lady's temple, and they come expressing the god's anger and disapproval, with warnings to stop the work.

I was present when they made this appeal yesterday, and I said: "In truth this Elohi you worship was the son of the Allmother and the consort of her Daughters. He brought disaster on Her people by flood and fire in order to bring them to the worship of himself. He it was who drove the people out of Great Nammu's Pleasure Garden. He rules through cruelty. Those who make their sacrifices to him—even you priests—do so out of fear, whereas we love our generous Lady with all our hearts. Renounce your allegiance to this harsh lord and the Lady Asherah will protect you from his anger." This speech enraged them.

I have advised the priests that we can worship in our separate ways and places without enmity. But they see how much their worshippers are drawn back to Lady Asherah because of my presence, and they resist all such approaches. They stand in the streets prophesying evil.

LETTER 3

To the most holy Ishnat, Queen of Tyre and Sidon, High Priestess of the Holy Shrines, Beloved of the Lady Asherah, daughter of Banab, High Priestess and Queen of Tyre and Sidon, descended through four hundred and five generations from Asherah, Daughter of the Great Goddess Yahu, from her loving and obedient daughter Yahzebul, High Priestess and Queen of Israel.

Honoured Mother,

By the Lady's grace, my daughter Athaliya arrived safe and well, and there has been much rejoicing in the kingdom. Ahab is delighted with her, and for her part she smiles at him and clings to his beard. At the consecration, the Lady was pleased with her, and the omens were good.

The building of the new temple is progressing well, and Ahab is determined to please the Lady.

He has ordered many other building works for the benefit of the people. He wants to improve the city, and at his command engineers are fashioning pipes to bring fresh water into the city, as well as stone-set roads that will be passable in all seasons.

My own concern has been to repair the tree and hill shrines that the Elohist priests have desecrated. In some, the sacred rites have not been performed for moons. This is a source of distress among Her worshippers, some of whom have to travel long distances to make offerings or sacrifice. I have ordered that all be repaired and cleansed and as each is ready, I go with our Congress Priestesses and Priests to re-dedicate them. This the people greatly approve. The vandalism has now been much reduced too, for they see that we restore the shrines immediately.

At Ahab's command, the port at Dor is being expanded. Soon half of the journey between us may be accomplished by sea, and I hope that this will bring you to visit at an early date.

LETTER 4

To the most holy Ishnat, Queen of Tyre and Sidon, High Priestess of the Holy Shrines, Beloved of the Lady Asherah, from her loving and obedient daughter Yahzebul, High Priestess and Queen of Israel.

My beloved Mother,
My son Ahaziah is born. Ahab was well pleased, for he foresees that my son will follow him in the kingship in due course. He announced a festival of celebration, and the people feasted and rejoiced.

But the omens were not good. My Prophecy Priestess warned:

When the king breaks his bond
The young king is too soon
The house falls
Its children will be slaves
For a hundred generations

Ahab was angry when he heard it, demanding another reading, but the Priestess was silent. I said to him, "It is not worthwhile to be angry. Prophecy is a guide, never a certainty until you make it so." But in truth I fear that prophecy only comes to those who are unable to benefit from it.

LETTER 5

To the most holy Ishnat, Queen of Tyre and Sidon, High Priestess of the Holy Shrines, Beloved of the Lady Asherah, daughter of Banab, High Priestess and Queen of Tyre and Sidon, descended through four hundred and five generations from Asherah, Daughter of the Great Goddess Yahu, from her loving and obedient daughter Yahzebul, High Priestess and Queen of Israel.

The Lady's temple is now complete, my beloved Mother. It stands on the highest point of the city, and its white marble and ivory glory may be seen from a vast distance all around. My consort has spared nothing in creating its beauty. Great was the wonder and rejoicing at the consecration.

Great too was the joy and amazement when your gifts arrived. The line of laden asses, and especially the elephant (who, the drovers told me, had to be tied down in the ship, for her least movement might have sunk them!) drew all the city into the streets to cheer and wonder. We have housed her in the public gardens among the ornamental pools, where she delights in spraying water on those who come to gaze at her.

When the beasts were unloaded and the gifts carried into the temple, we wept for the beauty. Such an array of golden statues, hangings, icons, basins, painted tiles, pitchers, and love ornaments!

And oh! The wonderful art of the Holy Cup that you have had made for our Vulva-Blood sacrament! My Priestesses were silent with awe. Our metal workers here have yet to produce anything so fine.

84

The golden statue of the Great Lady I brought with me at my marriage now graces the East wall of the great Communal Worship Hall. The tapestries depicting the sacred postures of Asherah and her consort, so skillfully crafted by your palace artists, hang on the walls there and provoke wonder and admiration in all who come.

The Elohist temple is a mud hut in comparison. Our temple is a great evil to the Elohist priests, for they can plainly see that the Lady Asherah draws many back to Her worship. They nurse the hope that the fury of their pronouncements against me will prevent this. So they prophesy doom for the whole kingdom if Asherah's Holy House is not pulled down. But the people love and trust the Lady to hold them safe.

You ask what draws the Elohi-worshippers on. I can only say that the Elohists are a people used to hardship, and accept it as a just punishment for what they call *sin*. They work hard on the land and with their animals, and who can say why their lord sends them so much disappointment?

Their crops fail, their sheep miscarry, their olives drop before harvest, even their bees disappear and do not return to the hive. These are hardship enough, but while Our Lady opens the storerooms of her temple, so that the offerings which the people made in times of plenty feed them in difficult times, no such succour is there for those who worship Elohi.

Even those who have had the wisdom to set aside stores against such a chance must surrender their hoard to the temple and go hungry. The priests say this is ordered by Elohi to placate his anger, but it is no surprise if they hear Elohi say so. Some of the Elohists do wonder at this, some have returned to the Lady and thrown off all the marks of their former allegiance. But very many shoulder the burden in silence to show their obedience. They take it as a mark of pride that Elohi brings suffering upon them, in the hope that he will reward them afterwards for their devotion.

LETTER 6

To the most holy Ishnat, Queen of Tyre and Sidon, High Priestess of the Holy Shrines, Beloved of the Lady Asherah, daughter of Banab, High Priestess and Queen of Tyre and Sidon, descended through four hundred and five generations from Asherah, Daughter of the Great Goddess Yahu, from her loving and obedient daughter Yahzebul, High Priestess and Queen of Israel.

W ise and most wise Mother,
I must tell you of one very troublesome priest, worse than all the rest, and ask your advice about him. His name is Eli-xha, "dedicated to Elohi" in their language. We call him El-Lexhi, God-Jawbone, because he shouts so furiously. This name infuriates him, but he does worse to my own name[14]. He demands respect but gives none.

He is given to fits of rage that he pretends are prophetic trance. He denounces me daily in the street as a witch and *harlot*, the word the Elohi priests use to describe our Congress Priestesses—whom they hate most when they have secretly worshipped with them. Elijaw froths at the mouth like one of those thirst-crazed madmen who come in from the desert swearing they've seen the heavenly city, but he commands attention from many. They see his state as divine trance, and he is becoming stronger.

Elijaw is relentless in his angry pursuit of Ahab, regularly accosting him in the street or, most often, at the gates of Asherah's temple, to promise him that Elohi will destroy his house. He sometimes challenges me directly, though he seems mostly afraid to do so. The wisdom snakes become agitated whenever he is in our presence, and he avoids me when he knows they are with me.

He is braver at other times. Once he asked this senseless question: "How many of Jizzabel's children are Ahab's seed?" He likes to pretend he can't pronounce my name, giving it a crude meaning in his Tishbite dialect.

I replied, "My children are my seed, Elijaw, as well you know. If a man had seed, he would give birth himself."

Those listening laughed. I said, "Even Elohists must know how foolish it is to talk of a man's seed. When has a man ever given birth? When has he ever spilled his sweetwater on the ground and seen it germinate? Even in your own stories Elohi does not talk of his *seed*, but of his *word*. Let us see you, holy man, utter a word and afterwards give birth. 'Let there be life!'"

He screeched more blasphemies, spitting into his beard, and went off with a small group of followers. It is a matter of pride with these prophets that they are filthy and ragged. I am sure they crawl with vermin. They consider such bodily uncleanness 'holy', perhaps because with us cleanliness is a mark of respect to Our Lady. Who would perform the sacred rites for her, if our Congress Priestesses and Congress Priests neglected the duty to bathe?

LETTER 7

To the most holy Ishnat, Queen of Tyre and Sidon, High Priestess of the Holy Shrines, descended through four hundred and five generations from Asherah, Daughter of the Great Goddess Yahu, from her loving and obedient daughter Yahzebul, High Priestess and Queen of Israel.

Our best greetings to you at this season of celebration, my beloved Mother.

I thank you for your warning as to coming drought. With so much advance warning, I am as hopeful as you that we will be able to prepare for it. Construction has already begun on the new temple storage barn here in Shamar, and I have sent instructions to my priestesses in every city and town.

I have received the Lady's approval for the changes now ordained. Though it is a hardship, her people are obeying without complaint the demand for increased offerings of grain, honey, oil, vegetables, and dried fruits. We also withhold from live offerings and the herds are increasing. We will ask the Lady's permission to suspend the communal worship at the Great Festival, for those who are pregnant or breastfeeding will suffer greatly when the rains stop.

This in haste.

89

LETTER 8

To the most holy Ishnat, Queen of Tyre and Sidon, High Priestess of the Holy Shrines, Beloved of the Lady Asherah, from her loving and obedient daughter Yahzebul. In haste.

T he rains have stopped, my Mother, as your dream foretold. We received none of the usual Naruju and Upara rains and the skies remain cloudless.

Elijaw has learned of the drought from his god very late. He warned Ahab of it a few weeks ago, when the signs were already clear, saying it was a punishment from Elohi. He told Ahab the only way to avert famine was to tear down the temple. Then he fled into the hill country, perhaps fearing that his people would demand his intercession with Elohi.

Ahab came to me in a worry, saying, "What can we do about this, is there any other way to prevent this drought?" So foolish are men, even those called kings.

I said, "Even Elohi cannot prevent this drought now. The coffers and storage barns of all the Asherah temples throughout your land are well stocked, and our people will not suffer as much as you fear. Direct your worry to the Elohists, for their temple priests have taken no precautions, in spite of my warnings, and it is now too late."

Elijaw is at worst a fraud, at best a conjuror, but it is clear that his constant threats of punishment worry my consort, and I fear for the Lady's shrines and sacred spaces. How I would welcome your advice on what to do about this troublesome man, my wise mother.

LETTER 9

To the most holy Ishnat, Queen of Tyre and Sidon, High Priestess of the Holy Shrines, Beloved of the Lady Asherah, daughter of Banab, High Priestess and Queen of Tyre and Sidon, descended through four hundred and five generations from Asherah, Daughter of the Great Goddess Yahu, from her loving and obedient daughter Yahzebul, High Priestess and Queen of Israel.

Most wise beloved Mother,
The drought continues here, as you say it does with you. We have done all that was ordained and approved by the Lady and advised by you. The people now see the benefit of such foresight and bless the Lady for her wisdom and generosity. None go without save the Elohists, whose children beg piteously in the streets and at our temple door.

Many springs have failed now. By our Lady's grace, the one feeding the city through the pipes my consort built still flows. Once the people have drawn water for their needs, we direct it into the ritual pool, where the Congress Priestesses and Priests have usually enough to bathe. Those with an urgent wish for worship may bathe with them. So the temple continues to sweeten the Allmother's dreams a little, though full communal worship has long been suspended.

From the ritual pool the water is directed to the animal pens, where the people can also collect a little for their household animals. The large flocks have long since failed. As you advised, the animals were sacrificed to the Lady as the fodder ran out, so as our stores of vegetables and grains decline, we are able to distribute more meat. A quantity still remains in our smokehouses and with the Lady's blessing it will last until the rains return.

Among the Elohists, only the priests are still eating. They remain plump and oiled while their people scrabble the parched earth for any seed or insect to eat. They look like insects themselves. Some of our people are still able to feed the Elohist children. But there is great hardship; the fields are burnt and brown and the trees fail to leave.

May it rain again soon.

LETTER 10

To the most holy Ishnat, Queen of Tyre and Sidon, High Priestess of the Holy Shrines, Beloved of the Lady Asherah, daughter of Banab, High Priestess and Queen of Tyre and Sidon, descended through four hundred and five generations from Asherah, Daughter of the Great Goddess Yahu, from her loving and obedient daughter Yahzebul, High Priestess and Queen of Israel.

Honoured Mother,
I bow nine times to you and to the Lady Asherah. We have had rain for four days. All are celebrating with the utmost joy. On the third day, which was Lady Day, we rejoiced with our first communal offering and sent great love and pleasure to the Lady. I hope your own worship has been as joyful.

With the rain has returned the one who describes himself as Elohi's prophet. Elijaw disappeared for the whole time of the drought. Now he has come and announced himself. The man looks robust, it seems he suffered little hardship in the famine. I have no doubt a family starved their children to feed this priest. Ahab was angry at the sight of him, but Elijaw is unrepentant.

He was loud in blaming the famine on Elohi's anger with those who worship in the hill shrines and at Our Lady's temple. I laughed at this and said, "Those who worshipped with us also ate with us, Elijaw. The Lady protects those who love Her from the vengeance of Elohi."

He is surely worried about the situation: he has now invited me to a mutual worship of the Lady Asherah and Elohi. I hope that he has been, however briefly, chastened by the sight of so many of his people thin and desperate, and I have deemed it wise to agree to it.

Still, he says nothing which I believe. The Lady warns of treachery. He named the hill shrine on Mount Ebal, and we agreed on an auspicious day. I will be on my guard.

LETTER 11

To the most holy Ishnat, Queen of Tyre and Sidon, High Priestess of the Holy Shrines, Beloved of the Lady Asherah, daughter of Banab, High Priestess and Queen of Tyre and Sidon, descended through four hundred and five generations from Asherah, Daughter of the Great Goddess Yahu, from her loving and obedient daughter Yahzebul, High Priestess and Queen of Israel.

A ll-seeing Mother,
It grieves me to tell you that your warning arrived too late. The effect of my error in trusting Elijaw even so little as I did has been disastrous, and I will not soon forget it. Behold the perfidy of this prophet of perfidious Elohi.

On Dark Moon Day of Upara, I went with my Priestesses, and every priest-consort except twenty young Baal novitiates, to re-consecrate the shrine on Mount Gerez after the long suspension. We went out of the city among much rejoicing, for the people are delighted to have the sacred sites restored to use.

Early the next morning Elijaw gathered his priests and a crowd and led them to our temple. Pretending ignorance of our absence, he loudly announced the mutual worship we had agreed upon. As if this were the agreed date, he called for me to join him instantly with my Priestesses to set off for Mount Ebal.

The Baal novitiates, children that they were, went out to explain that all were absent. The mad prophet began to rail and mock, accusing me of fearing to present Asherah before Elohi. The boys were confused, protesting that we would return before evening.

Elijaw then pretended to fall into a prophetic fit and in a loud, threatening voice declared that the joint worship should happen immediately or Asherah's worshippers would be cursed forever. He cried out that the novitiates themselves should take my place at the mutual worship.

"Why do you fear to show us the power of him you worship?" he shouted, and those with him began to jeer.

The Baal novitiates resisted, saying no such worship could happen without me. Elijaw humiliated them before the people, saying they were afraid because their god was weak. Some in the crowd began to chant in derision and throw shit and stones.

One of the novitiates resisted even this, saying to the others that it was a trick and they should not go. But Elijaw continued to mock them, and a larger crowd gathered and at last all but the one agreed to go with him and his baying mob.

The following I learned from two who afterwards escaped: when they set off carrying a Baal icon from the temple, Elijaw led them not to the appointed hill shrine, but to another spot on Mount Ebal, and directed them where to set down the icon opposite his own altar. They built an altar in front of the icon and broke branches to lay on it, while the crowd mocked them for their lack of preparation. Then the priests brought in two young bulls and Elijaw demanded that they choose one.

All the novitiates protested that they were not yet consecrated and could not undertake to slaughter a bull for an offering to Baal. They could offer only field fruits. Elijaw mocked them, but none would engage in such blasphemy. Then with great fanfare Elijaw slaughtered the bull himself, cut it up, laid it on their altar and demanded that they summon Baal himself to light the offering.

The novitiates were distressed and confused, not knowing how to leave without the Baal icon, but prevented from leaving with it, for by Elijaw's command, the priests kept them away from the altar. He kept on demanding that they summon Baal to light the flame. The crowd were by now pushing and pulling them, mocking their robes and hair, snatching at their necklaces.

No one listened to their protest that it was the task of worshippers to light offerings to Baal. Out of fear the boys began to perform the ritual dances they were learning, while the crowd jeered.

Elijaw dragged forward the other bull, slaughtered it and placed it on his own altar. Then from among his priests were produced buckets full of liquid; he directed them to pour it over his sacrifice.

"Water!" he cried to the crowd. "We will soak our offering to Elohi in water!" And when the buckets were empty, with a great show he waved the priests at what he called a spring, and they gathered more liquid and poured it over the altar.

Know, my Mother, that there is a source of *burning-water* on Mount Ebal. In summer flame often dances there. He soaked the offering not with water, but with that strange fire-loving liquid. Some of the assembled must have known of it; children love to climb up in summer and throw sticks into the flames.

Then Elijaw began to call on Elohi, begging him to himself set light to the offering, to prove to the assembled which was the stronger god. One of my two survivors says he saw Elijaw toss something at the altar, which burst into flame with a thunderous roar.

The assembled were inspired with terror and wonder at this manifestation, some of them our own people who repented loudly their worship of The Lady and Baal. They fell on their faces, crying, "This is the true god!"

Elijaw pointed at my novitiates crying, "They are evil-doers who anger your god! Seize them! Let none escape!"

These children, some only nine years old, and none over fourteen, were chased down the mountain by the mob, and slaughtered before they reached Shechem. I have heard that Elijaw bragged of murdering three of them by his own hand.

When we returned from our ceremony on Mount Gerez, we were met with two who had escaped by hiding in a small cave. We took three chariots and went and gathered the Baal and the bodies of the seventeen who were murdered, all still lying wherever they had fallen.

As the chariots returned to Shamar the mothers of the boys came out to meet them and set up a wailing that alerted all the city. People came to see and even the Elohists were horrified by the slaughter their priests had committed, and cried out upon their own.

The priests said, "We had a sign, we were given a sign!" and tried to avoid their shame.

Elijaw has fled again. Against children he is a brave assassin. But he is wise to be afraid of my vengeance. Be assured that this villainy will not go unpunished.

LETTER 12

To the most holy Ishnat, Queen of Tyre and Sidon, High Priestess of the Holy Shrines, Beloved of the Lady Asherah, daughter of Banab, High Priestess and Queen of Tyre and Sidon, descended through four hundred and five generations from Asherah, Daughter of the Great Goddess Yahu, from her loving and obedient daughter Yahzebul, High Priestess and Queen of Israel.

D ear and wise Mother,
Ahab is dead. He was killed in one of his fruitless border wars. After only three years, he violated the peace with Aram that my sister Queen Yahzuna and I arranged between our two consorts, and this is the price.

I was in Yizreel after the death of my High Priestess there when word came to me that Judah son of Queen Azubah had arrived in Shamar with his army in full battle array. He goaded Ahab into a renewed sense of outrage over villages and vineyards near Gil'ad that had been the source of a longstanding dispute between Aram and ourselves.

I could not leave Yizreel before anointing a new High Priestess, but sent a message forbidding such treachery. When all was acceptable to the Great Lady, I returned in haste to Shamar. These two warlords had donned their armour and mustered their armies and only then consulted the Elohist prophets, with great public fanfare. They all, to a man, had advised that Elohi loved war and would deliver them the victory. As I arrived, those who had witnessed this foolishness were in the streets cheering and chanting: "Ramot-Gil'ad is ours! Ramot-Gil'ad for the Lord!"

I confronted Ahab in the palace, where he was instructing servants to polish his armour for the planned sortie. I forbade him to violate the agreement with Aram and our sister, but he was full of Elohist bloodlust and only said he should never have agreed to give up land which Elohi had designated as his own.

Then I was given prophecy and the Lady spoke a warning:

> *They will be like sheep after a storm*
> *Scattered over the wet grass*
> *Lost and calling for their king*
> *But you too will be one of the lost*
> *Alive or dead*

Ahab said only, "Make that prediction to Aram!"

The Goddess departed, and I said to him, "Well, I see you will go. But let me advise you not to wear your bright king's armour into battle, for as you are violating a sacred pact with Aram, he will certainly mark you out as a target. Do not count on any courtesy from him should you be captured, but it is more likely that you will be killed outright. I will crown my son Ahaziah in your stead. But he is unready, and you are a fool to leave your kingdom at such risk, for some will surely see his youth as weakness."

Even this did not sway him; he was ever a man whose blood clouded his brain. They brought home his corpse this morning. He had worn the armour of an ordinary commander, they told me, but at the last minute he could not bear to leave off the bright helmet and warlord's plume.

I will crown my son Ahaziah immediately, and I beg you to send him a bride to validate his kingship as soon as you can. But I fear that nothing can now undo the fate forewarned of in the prophecy at my son's birth.

LETTER 13

To the most holy Ishnat, Queen of Tyre and Sidon, High Priestess of the Holy Shrines, Beloved of the Lady Asherah, daughter of Banab, High Priestess and Queen of Tyre and Sidon, descended through four hundred and five generations from Asherah, Daughter of the Great Goddess Yahu, from her loving and obedient daughter Yahzebul, High Priestess and Queen of Israel.

M ost honoured Mother,
Elijaw has reappeared, now hourly prophesying disaster for my son's reign, as a punishment for Ahab's lifelong worship of the Lady Asherah.

The man is old and enfeebled in everything except his violent speech and the amount of spittle that comes from his mouth when he prophesies. And now he is accompanied by a handsome young man he calls his disciple and heir.

Rumour says the young man is the son of a woman who housed Elijaw twenty years ago and gave him congress. By the strange rules of the Elohists they call him Elijaw's son, though he never showed a father's care. Others, however, say the boy is his lover. The first rumour I can easily believe: these priests and prophets condemn our pleasure worship without themselves abstaining. The second seems to me unlikely, for Elijaw is surely too feeble now even to have a thought of congress worship.

In spite of this, my son Ahaziah is much disturbed by the doom the man promises, and has asked me if Elohi could overpower the will of Lady Asherah and bring such

horrors as Elijaw promises upon his head. I consulted the
Lady in his presence, and he received this prophecy:

So long as Goddess light shines bright upon you
You are safe
The sun is your protector
Do not greet the babbler of evil fates
Within house or palace, within your tent
Or at night
His strength lies in the shadows

But he is not comforted. The power of these priests
grows here; the fear of Elohi's wrath is a miasma spreading
through the air, choking all who breathe it in. I therefore
beg your advice: how to soothe my son's fears and protect
him from this pollution?

LETTER 14

To the most holy Ishnat, Queen of Tyre and Sidon, High Priestess of the Holy Shrines, Beloved of the Lady Asherah, from her loving and obedient daughter Yahzebul, High Priestess and Queen of Israel.

D earest Mother,
Your wisdom was perfect as ever, but my son was not perfect enough to follow it. Ahaziah heard Elijaw shouting in the street outside the palace and sent a man to summon him within. Who can say why? He went to his upper terrace and placed himself at the furthest corner from the entry, in full sunlight, believing that that was sufficient obedience to the Lady and yourself.

But the instant the prophet stepped into the space, so filthy that he left contamination in his wake, he rushed at my son, waving his arms and shouting curses. Ahaziah's people afterwards told me that this apparition was terrifying, and in his shock Ahaziah leapt backwards. The latticework gave way and he fell down onto the roof of his council chamber, from where they had great trouble bringing him down, his spine and head being injured.

Elijaw fled again at my approach, and went up into the hills with his disciple, but he is old, and they moved slowly. Two of my priests, acting without instruction, followed him to his lair. I rewarded them then, but afterwards wished that he had been allowed to escape to the wilderness unremarked.

My son was deeply disturbed in his mind, as well as suffering great pain, and insisted I send to an oracle to know if he would live. I sent to Magad, and also the Great Oracle at Akko, because while I believed he would recover, he was so disturbed in mind that nothing else would calm him.

But this was not enough for Ahaziah, who in his delirium insisted on hearing what Elijaw would prophesy. What can explain the hold this madman has over men? I told Ahaziah that the man had fled, and we didn't know where. But he had overheard my priests tell me that they had followed Elijaw to his lair. He could not rest and, bad as it would be to bring the man in to make his evil prophesies, I could see that my son would fret himself to death before the messenger returned even from Magad.

I hoped that if my son's bed were carried into the open air it would be safe. So I sent men to bring Elijaw down from his lair, and down he came, and told my son that his death was certain. Two days after he died, the message from Magad arrived, saying that only if the prophet of Elohi was not admitted to his presence indoors or out would Azahiah recover.

Ahaziah was my first son and I loved him dearly. I know that without the influence of that mad priest he would be alive now. It is an unforgivable crime, and you may be sure I do not forgive it.

LETTER 15

To the most holy Ishnat, Queen of Tyre and Sidon, High Priestess of the Holy Shrines, Beloved of the Lady Asherah, daughter of Banab, High Priestess and Queen of Tyre and Sidon, descended through four hundred and five generations from Asherah, Daughter of the Great Goddess Yahu, from her loving and obedient daughter Yahzebul, High Priestess and Queen of Israel.

Beloved Mother,

At last I am rid of that foul prophet.

He tried to escape, but my people tracked him so that at all times I knew where he was. I sent my priests to Mount Ebal with a large urn well-fixed in a chariot and bade them fill the urn with burning-water from the source there, which they had much trouble to do.

The next time a runner came in to tell me where Elijaw was, he had left Yariho and was on the road to Gilgal. Four of my Priestesses, two in the chariot with the urn, and two in a chariot behind with a small firepot, set off early.

Crossing at the Gilgal ford, they found the prophet and his disciple just at nightfall, heading towards Sittim. My Priestesses in the lead chariot drove it to stop beside him.

The young man wisely fled, but Elijaw was too feeble for that, and they gave him this: "We bring greetings from the Lady Yahzebul to the regicide-priest Elijaw. May even your own god not forgive your foul crime. Let you call on that god now for salvation, if you think it possible, for those who live by fire, shall they not die by fire?"

I am told that he sniffed the air as he looked up at them and there was stark fear in his eyes. He gazed out over the desert hills but knew he could not hope to escape. "Spare me," he begged. "I am an old man and will soon die."

My Priestesses only said, as instructed, "Do you ask for mercy, who have never granted it?"

They tell me in supplication he even pressed his hands together in Closed Vulva, as if She Herself might be called on by such as he. "Cut my throat first," he begged, even as they began to dip jugs of the burning-water from the urn, pouring it over his head and body while he coughed and choked.

"Call on your god, Elijaw," they cried. "If he has the power to ignite water at your command, surely he can also refuse to ignite it? Summon him, summon great Elohi, as you did on Mount Ebal! Let it be known that he is lord!"

When the urn was empty, they moved the chariot ahead, leaving him drenched, matted hair and rough sandals and robe.

By this time darkness had fallen. The second chariot had stopped at a distance. When the first was well clear, they galloped towards Elijaw, who stood at the side of the road blinded and helpless.

They passed at speed, then flung a burning coal back into the pool at his feet. The roar of the burning-water igniting and his tortured scream combined to cause the horses to bolt, or my Priestesses might have been injured, so hot and intense, they tell me, was the eruption. As it was, it ignited the chariot's four standing torches and the hair of my priestess Ahaval.

They stopped at a distance to marvel at the inferno that burned him, for the fire reached many cubits into the night sky and lighted the hills all around as if it were day. When there was nothing left but charcoaled bones the chariots went on to Sittim. And so I am rid at last of this villainous man.

Word has come that the prophet's disciple, who ran up into the hills and watched from a distance, reported in wonder and amaze that Elijaw "went up to Lord Elohi in a pillar of fire".

May Elohi approve my burnt offering!

LETTER 16

*To the most holy Ishnat, Queen of Tyre and Sidon, High Priestess
of the Holy Shrines, Beloved of the Lady Asherah, daughter of
Banab, High Priestess and Queen of Tyre and Sidon, descended
through four hundred and five generations from Asherah, Daughter
of the Great Goddess Yahu, from her loving and obedient daughter
Yahzebul, High Priestess and Queen of Israel.*

H onoured beloved Mother,
Jehoram was never the son of my heart, but what
was I to do? My other sons were all too young, and the
Israelites must have a King-Warlord at all times. There
were many contenders for the kingship among the sons of
Ahab's other wives. These women were arguing among
themselves over which one should have precedence, but I
was not such a fool as to imagine they would not soon
agree.

Jehoram is in every way an Elohist. The damage was
done too early to be undone. After one of my visits to you,
I returned to Shamar to discover that Ahab had allowed
Jehoram to be taken away to study with Elohist priests.
Some prophet had issued a warning and, as always, Ahab
was unsettled by fear. It was three years before I could
recover my son. By then they had filled the boy's head
with such fear of their angry, bloodthirsty lord, and such
filthy hatred for divine Asherah, that he never recovered.

When he came of age, we took him to the temple to
be consecrated to the Allmother's service, and he told me
afterwards that he had been *defiled* and that the Congress
Priestess was a *harlot*. Yahu's rage consumed me, and I

whipped him with a chariot rein. From that moment there has been enmity between us.

Jehoram has accepted no counsel from me since the day I crowned him. He has all the Elohist taste for making war, and loves nothing more than to muster his army and go off to despoil a neighbour.

As you have heard, all who live along our borders are at risk—Ammon, Aram, and any of the tiny fiefdoms whose borders march with ours. He even takes pride in driving off the nomadic tribes who have always passed through the lands without trouble. He loses many of his own soldiers in these fruitless battles, but cares not for that.

Most of these attacks are inspired by some priest or other. The worst of them is that same disciple of Elijaw whom I have mentioned before—he who calls himself God's Saviour. Eliash loves bloodshed and will always encourage Jehoram with promises of god-given victory. And whenever Jehoram loses a battle or his forces suffer heavy losses, he is sure to order the destruction of at least one of our hill shrines and the sacred pillars, saying that the defeat was a punishment from Elohi for allowing Our Lady's worship to continue in the land.

Now this prophet's eye has fallen upon Moab, our Goddess-loving ally by the Salt Sea. The people cultivate olives in abundance. They are also rich in sheep. They pay good tribute to us every year for protection and have no standing army.

Jehoram's pretext for this attack is this: Moab has not sent his full tribute in wool for several years, under the excuse that disease has been killing his sheep.

I have told my son that Asherah not only disapproves but also promises disaster from such an expedition against a protected ally. I have reminded him that there still stands a hill shrine at Yarosaleem commemorating this treaty. He disdains to listen. He has even invited the warlords of Judah and Edom to join forces with him in this expedition, and they surely will.

The Lady warns not only of disaster to Jehoram in this battle, but also of grave danger to me and my children as a result. I ask for your valued advice: is there any way to stop my son?

LETTER 17

To the most holy Ishnat, Queen of Tyre and Sidon, High Priestess of the Holy Shrines, Beloved of the Lady Asherah, daughter of Banab, High Priestess and Queen of Tyre and Sidon, descended through four hundred and five generations from Asherah, Daughter of the Great Goddess Yahu, from her loving and obedient daughter Yahzebul, High Priestess and Queen of Israel.

W isest of women, my beloved Mother,
I wrote to our sister the High Priestess Queen Misya in Moab, with advice to her consort King Hobab, as you advised. He could hardly believe the warning, but he sent out scouts, and when they returned with the news that Jehoram, Judah, and Edom were mustering their armies in the wilderness of Edom, he summoned his citizens to assemble at the border with Edom. Women, men, and children all responded. A few had bows and arrows, even fewer spears and swords. Some were armed with hammers or rakes, some with nothing but their field-measuring sticks. None had armour or shield.

The following news I have received from my scouts, and also from a soldier in Jehoram's army.

The Moabite citizens' army was overrun in an hour. Those who were not quick enough to flee were slaughtered, women, men, children even of the age of seven. Then these three brave armies marched North through Moab, setting fire to orchards and crops, smashing the desalination and irrigation works. They burned villages and wantonly slaughtered sheep. They violated the dead bodies of their victims.

Their bloodlust was spurred on by Jehoram's priest Eliash, who travelled with them and shouted as they pillaged and burned that the destruction was at Elohi's command. Who can understand the mystery of this god who so loves death, or those who worship him?

The armies moved down towards the capital for three days, sleeping only in snatches, eating what they pillaged before burning houses and fields and orchards, not stopping even to wash off the blood, spreading wide and killing all in their path. The towns of So-Ar and Luhit and Hornai were utterly razed—not a mouse left alive, even the smallest potted sapling uprooted. Then they came to the king's walled sacred city.

The Queen and King were in despair at this wanton destruction of their nation. With the murderous horde approaching, they believed that only a blood offering would placate Elohi. They stood upon the wall of the city in full view of the mob of soldiers, and Hobab with his own hands prepared to kill their only son.

In the terrible silence, for even blood-drunk monsters could be silenced by such a sight, the king called out, "Let your god take this most precious son as our sacrifice and let his bloodlust be sated here and stop the rest."

Our sister Misya's anguished cries as the young prince dutifully offered up his throat to his father's knife shamed them all, even as the sacrifice satisfied Elohi. His bloodlust left the armies, and without entering the gates of the city they turned and went back the way they had come.

They nearly starved on the way home, I am told, for they had destroyed every fruit tree, burned every olive hut, every granary; had choked the springs and stuffed the wells with dead bodies which were now rotting. Any scrap of food left from their pillaging was stinking with blood and thick with flies and dirt. Even such they tried to eat. They tore meat from the rotting carcasses of sheep they had slaughtered days before.

Jehoram came home blustering, pretending it had been a success, that he had 'subdued' King Hobab, calling it a punishment for the tribute shortfall.

I said, "What tribute will you get from him now? You have burned their orchards and slaughtered their sheep. How will they now send wool? It will be a nine-year cycle before you see a drop of oil or a single sheepskin from Moab.

"Furthermore, he has sacrificed his son to your god, and even while he pays tribute, he will be your enemy forever. Beware they do not send assassins to your own house—or yourself. This is the fool you are, this is the fool that your bloodthirsty prophet is, this is the fool of a god you worship."

He was angry that I knew so much, and said so much, and angrier still because he was ashamed. He tried to silence me. But prophecy entered me then, and revealed this:

> *The very prophet who urged you to the slaughter*
> > *will betray you*
> *He will anoint another in your place even while you live*
> *And his anointed one will assassinate you in your bed*
> *He will slaughter your brothers and sisters*
> *He will destroy Ahab's house root and branch*
> *In Shamar and in Yizreel and all the land of Israel.*

I have moved my court to Yizreel. And now I will act on your advice and begin to send my children and household to you in Tyre. I must be discreet, for if Eliash has knowledge of my intentions he will surely move quickly. Therefore, they will come by ones and twos, over time, in small trains, as if on a visit.

I will remain here to see the end of this.

LETTER 18

To the most holy Ishnat, Queen of Tyre and Sidon, High Priestess of the Holy Shrines, Beloved of the Lady Asherah, daughter of Banab, High Priestess and Queen of Tyre and Sidon, descended through four hundred and five generations from Asherah, Daughter of the Great Goddess Yahu, from her loving and obedient daughter Yahzebul, High Priestess and Queen of Israel.

W isest of women, my Mother,
We have just had the news that Eliash has anointed as king his own kinsman. Ben-Nimshi is undistinguished, a mere army captain. Treachery I have been expecting since the Lady's warning, but this is a strange, incomprehensible choice, and my spies tell me that even many Elohists are dubious about how it came to be.

We have learned that a messenger from Eliash went to Ben-Nimshi when he was dining with a group of captains and took him into a private room. When Ben-Nimshi appeared again he announced that he had been anointed king by the messenger, at the command of the prophet.

It is rumoured that this was a lie, but that once Ben-Nimshi had declared himself in this way, Eliash feared to contradict him. Who can know what really happened? But it is all the same to us. My son, Jehoram, is now at very grave risk.

All the family of Ahab—his wives and their children, his court, all his ministers—are at risk if Jehoram is assassinated. This I expect almost every moment, for the fool is off to start another war in Aram, in spite of the perilous situation his kingship is now in. If Eliash tells one of the soldiers that Elohi commands him to kill his king commander, he is sure to be obeyed. Jehoram is not one who has given his retinue cause for loyalty.

I am glad to have your news that my daughters, Obediah and Salafi, have separately made their way to you, each with her family and household and valuables. That is a great comfort. Athaliya, Queen of Judah, has advised me that she will remain.

I will send you news as soon as I receive it. I will have it almost before Eliash himself, for any of his ragged train can be bought for a gold ring.

LETTER 19

To the most holy Ishnat, Queen of Tyre and Sidon, High Priestess of the Holy Shrines, from her loving and obedient daughter Yahzebul. In haste.

W ise and most beloved Mother,
Jehoram has been injured in battle. They brought him to Yizreel, where I have treated his wounds and left him under the guard of his fellow war fool Ahaz. He will survive if he is allowed to. It is now urgent that I complete the evacuation of my household, and I have brought Yamoon and Irasana in a parade of laden asses to the healing shrine at Magad, outwardly to sacrifice for their brother's recovery. The asses carry as many of our household treasures as it was possible to remove without suspicion, for who knows how many in my household have been subverted by that priest?

They will set off for Dor before dawn. This letter will be brought to you by them, and the last of my close household. I commit their safety to the Lady.

Send to me as soon as they arrive, I beg. I return to Yizreel and my son.

LETTER 20

To the most holy Ishnat, Queen of Tyre and Sidon, High Priestess of the Holy Shrines, descended through four hundred and five generations from Asherah, Daughter of the Great Goddess Yahu, from her loving and obedient daughter Yahzebul, High Priestess and Queen of Israel.

Beloved Mother,
Ben-Nimshi went to Jehoram as soon as I was absent and murdered him on his sickbed. My son's brave nephew, Ahaz, apparently fled with all his retinue at the first sign of Ben-Nimshi's approach, leaving Jehoram without protection. He would have done better to stay and fight, for Ben-Nimshi followed after Ahaz as soon as he had murdered my son. I have no doubt of the outcome there. When he has dispatched Ahaz, he will return to me in Yizreel.

You were right to warn me of treachery. The form of it surprised me, but let no one fail to understand the blind stupidity of men. Yesterday on my return from Shamar two of my priests dragged a third before me, Delash by name, and told me that he had been trying to induce them to join him in a plot against my life. Delash fell to his knees and confessed that Ben-Nimshi had promised him a rich position in the Elohi priesthood if he and two or three others, whom he was supposed to enlist with similar enticements, would kill me on his command.

Even in my fury I could laugh at this. I said, "You fool, do you think they promote such as you to any position in the temple of Elohi? You are forbidden to set

119

foot even in the antechamber of the room that houses their high altar. Their word for you is *abomination*. If Ben-Nimshi did not kill you as soon as you had done the deed, which he surely planned, you would be despised among them."

He put his hands in Spread Vulva above his bent head, weeping bitterly. "In my madness I have betrayed you, Great Lady of Asherah," he said, "and truly death is preferable to life now."

I asked, "How were you to kill me? With poison, a knife?"

"I was to throw you down from your window when he arrived, as he gave the command."

"So be it," I said. "What you have plotted against me shall be turned against you." Again he begged forgiveness. I said, "You must ask the Lady directly; I will not intercede for you. To plot to kill your High Priestess and Queen is too high a crime."

We now await Ben-Nimshi. Keep the messengers who bring this with you. With the Lady's blessing, I will join you very soon.

LETTER 21

To the most holy Ishnat, Queen of Tyre and Sidon from her loving and obedient daughter Yahzebul. In haste.

Most beloved Mother,
I will be with you very soon. But I know you will be anxious and therefore send this messenger on ahead, to give you the earliest possible news of our success. Be assured I am safe.

We learned that Ben-Nimshi and his train would arrive late on Dark Moon Day—I am sure by the will of the Lady. I dressed in purple and gold, painted my eyes and face, arranged my hair with gold braid, gold also on my wrists and neck and ears, as if out of fear and respect for him.

We dressed Delash in similar robes, painted his face, arranged his hair. When night fell we ordered no lamps lit in the courtyard or my balcony; the only light came from within.

Ben-Nimshi arrived with a small troop of horse well after dark. I went out onto the upper balcony accompanied by my priests, and called down to him in the shadows.

"Well, Ben-Nimshi, you that are a regicide and the lowest among men, what do you want here?"

He did not answer me, but looked up and called, "Who is with me?" Two of my priests, Yupin and Ashar, gave the sign they had learned from Delash, and Ben-Nimshi said, just as we had been told, "Throw her down."

They seized my arms and, as if in struggle, we moved back inside my chamber. There on the floor was Delash, shivering in terror—a poor image of me, but the darkness was our friend. Yupin and Ashar pulled him up and dragged him screaming out onto the balcony and threw him over. He fell to the degrading death that had been intended for me.

Ben-Nimshi actually drove his horse to trample the body. To his delight, blood spattered the paving stones, the walls, his horse and trappings, his own boots. Then with a cry of triumph he entered my palace and commanded my lower servants—who all believed that I was dead, and were weeping and calling—to prepare a feast for himself and his men.

As soon as he was at his meal, my priests went out and gathered up Delash's broken body, for fear that in his triumph Ben-Nimshi might go out to examine it. They left one arm and hand, which was so broken no one could have said to whom it had belonged, and the back of his skull.

Then we took the secret passage to the west gate where a wool cart was waiting, and lay among the sheepskins as it made its way to Magad. At first light we will set off for Dor. I am eager to be with you again, most honoured and beloved Mother.

FROM THE ANNALS OF TYRE AND SIDON

Dictated by Yahzebul, High Priestess of the Goddess Asherah, Great Queen of Tyre and Sidon, daughter of Ishnat, Queen of Tyre and Sidon, High Priestess of the Holy Shrines, granddaughter of Banab, High Priestess and Queen of Tyre and Sidon, descended through four hundred and six generations from Asherah, daughter of the Great Goddess Yahu, Queen of Heaven, dedicated to the service of the Goddess of the High Holiness, Queen of Heaven. Inscribed at her command by the Chief Scribe Dani

After my mother Ishnat, Queen of Tyre and Sidon and High Priestess of Asherah, died, I was consecrated High Priestess and Queen as had been ordained for me at my birth. My brother was then King of Tyre and Sidon.

Together we planned Ben-Nimshi's punishment, for Baal was so angered by the slaughter of the Lady's Priestesses and Priests and the defilement of the temple which Ben-Nimshi committed following my departure, he would be satisfied only with the downfall of the whole nation.

It was clear to us that Ben-Nimshi was too puffed up by his false kingship to remember the duties of his position. Elohi, or his priest Eliash, had chosen as king a man who shared their powerful bloodlust and high taste for the slaughter of innocents, but who was a weak commander.

In addition to the murder of every one of Ahab's wives and their children, Ben-Nimshi executed all our supervisory staff, including the commanders of every enterprise, from palace maintenance to irrigation to garrison supply, fodder storage, and even the pottery. In their places he appointed fools and friends with no experience and no interest in anything but graft and extortion.

Nor could he win the loyalty of the people or his troops. They knew he was a regicide and a usurper, whatever Eliash said.

He failed to maintain vital protection on his borders: many of his garrisoned soldiers were left without supplies and had to fend for themselves for long periods. Instead of manning the outposts they were seen begging work from farmers or trading in the villages of Aram, Ammon, Bashan and even Moab. Some were left so long without supplies that they traded their armaments for food.

These reports soon reached the ears of foreign kings, though not, it seemed, Ben-Nimshi's own drunken ears. He was proud of his murder of me (as he believed) and of Ahab's household, and bragged about the destruction of Asherah's temple and the assassination of my Priestesses.

We heard that he spent many nights dictating to a scribe so that the story of these great deeds should enter the annals of the kings, (as I dictate this so that the true story may be known). He did this at the evening meal, while all the company hid their yawns and dutifully applauded the lies, for it was soon rumoured that I was alive.

Some began to say openly that Ben-Nimshi's account of his anointing was also a lie, and that the lackey had delivered him a different message. Others said that Ben-Nimshi had threatened or bribed Eliash.

Whatever the truth of this, many great deeds and impossible magics of Eliash also entered the record during those evenings, for when Ben-Nimshi tired or fell to eating again, or dropped into a drunken stupor, Eliash would recount his own miraculous exploits, and the scribes would keep writing.

Meanwhile, the King and I made our plans.

Ammon and Bashan had standing armies, but by far the largest and strongest nation was Aram. We therefore sent the following embassy to Hazael, King of Aram.

Those of us who worship the Great Queen of Heaven should work together against the man and the nation that have killed so many of Her Priestesses and Priests and despoiled the great temple to Her honour built by King Ahab. Aram is a mighty power and her king a great warrior. Tyre is weak in armies but strong in wealth. We therefore propose a union between our two nations, for the better protection of the Goddess and Her Consort and Her sacred sites in all the nations devoted to Her worship.

We proposed that we should supply Aram with armaments from our workshops. In addition to house and farm implements, these workshops were dedicated to the manufacture of household gods and shrines, as well as bowls, statues, icons, and dedication objects for the Lady's temples. These craft workers could be diverted to the manufacture of arms.

Our embassy was successful. Hazael had taken good note of Ben-Nimshi's desecration of our holy places, as well as his mismanagement of the nation. He welcomed an alliance with us.

We consulted Asherah Queen of Heaven and gained the Lady's approval for this: that for five years there would be no new offerings of gold and silver in the temples, while her metal workers turned to the task of making armaments for Baal.

There was no complaining; our people rejoiced that the Lady would be avenged for the destruction of Her great temple at Shamar. Some of our pottery workshops began to produce fired ceramic copies of the usual offerings, with the name of the devotee inscribed, and these were brought to the temple as promise-offerings, to be replaced later with gold and silver. Many a daughter of Tyre and Sidon was consecrated to the Lady with only such promise-offerings, and it was considered no shame, and the Lady accepted all such.

We received word that Ben-Nimshi heard of his failure to kill me and my children but repudiated it. "I myself trampled her body till my horse's legs were bloodied up to the belly!" he screamed in one of the drunken fits that were all too common with him. "It is written in the annals of the kings!" As if everyone did not know that he had dictated those lies himself.

So I sent him this letter:

From Yahzebul, High Priestess of the Goddess Asherah and Her Consort Baal, Great Queen of Tyre and Sidon, daughter of Ishnat, Queen of Tyre and Sidon, High Priestess of the Holy Shrines, descended through four hundred and six generations from Asherah, daughter of the Great Goddess Yahu, to the regicide-usurper Ben-Nimshi.

Your foul deeds have grieved the Lady Asherah and enraged Her Consort Lord Baal. Your punishment at Lord Baal's hands will be to lose the kingdom you usurped; it will be torn from you piece by piece. Your nation will be dissolved and fall to other kings for all the generations to come. Such is the effect of your evil towards the Great Queen of Heaven. You will watch in helpless incompetence as your provinces fall, Gilad and Gad and Manasseh and Reuben, until you have nothing but the stolen palace at Shamar to reign over. You yourself will be humiliated and will bend the knee to a foreign king for the remaining years of your usurped kingship, and your people for a hundred generations will suffer under the yoke of harsh and cruel foreign kings. The nation you usurped will be nothing but an empty name. These are the fruits of your bloodthirsty evils which will never be wiped off. Behold the vengeance of the High Priestess Yahzebul on behalf of the Great Queen of Heaven. Prepare!

But he could not prepare. By the seventh year of his reign, when King Hazael was armed and ready, Ben-Nimshi's outposts were virtually unmanned. Many of his soldiers had abandoned them entirely, marrying into the tribes where they were stationed, turning themselves into farmers and sheepherders, shopkeepers and merchants, caring for the lands and flocks or shops and workshops of their wives, and above all, returning to their natural worship of the Lady Asherah.

Most of those remaining in the outposts were recruited into his own army by King Hazael on the promise of a steady wage, so that he marched in without resistance.

Ben-Nimshi was bluster to the last, for in his answer he at once denied that I was alive and cursed me to a degrading death.

In Shamar, meanwhile, the temple which he had used as a pisspot began to be cleared and rebuilt by the will of the worshippers. Ben-Nimshi was powerless even to protest. We sent labourers and supplies, marble and ivory, and finally Priestesses and Priests to cleanse the site of its defilement and re-consecrate it to the Lady.

The restoration of the temple is almost complete now. Ben-Nimshi still bends his knee to King Hazael and has given him much of the wealth of the Elohi temples, gold and silver, fine linens and woven wool, icons and caskets, all wrested from the unwilling hands of the priests. He pays tribute twice every year, and because he is so bad a manager, the tribute impoverishes the people.

Today I send him this:

From Yahzebul, High Priestess of the Goddess Asherah and her consort Baal, Great Queen of Tyre and Sidon, daughter of Ishnat, Queen of Tyre and Sidon, High Priestess of the Holy Shrines, descended through four hundred and six generations from Asherah, daughter of the Great Goddess Yahu, to the regicide-usurper Ben-Nimshi.

I am an old woman now, and you, I hear, are old in health if not in years. I know that you sit in my consort's palace in Shamar, besieged by the King of Aram on all sides, and do nothing but relive your history of assassinating Priestesses and kings, as if it were your pride instead of the deepest shame a man can confess to.

How desperate you were to be king, only you know. But how inadequate to the high position you craved and murdered for, all the world has seen these past twenty-five years. Because of your failings, the kingdom diminishes by the day, and you can only look forward and know that your son is not the man to reverse this. So I have my revenge on you, and I await my death with an easy heart.

THE PETITION OF ASHDIDA

Recorded by the Priestess-Scribe Yabuli on Devi Day of Allmother Week in Panjeh, the twenty-first year of the reign of the High Priestess Alyuni.

I am Ashdida, daughter of Ahora. I appeal for the intercession of the Lady and Her High Priestess in a dispute with an Elohist woman.

When I was a child my mother Ahora promised me to my cousin Baalit. A wild boar attacked Baalit while we were still children, and he died. When I was fifteen, I married Uzzi, the eldest son of an Elohist family who lived near us. His mother's name was Nomi, but he called himself son of Harim.

Both our families were satisfied with the match. Uzzi's sister told me that the Elohists like their sons to marry among us, because with us the daughters inherit the wealth of the mother. My mother owned fig and olive orchards, an olive mill, storage and drying barns, and large flocks, as well as tapestries and icons. Uzzi's father was a newcomer with little land. But he had gold, and two mules.

It was agreed between my mother and Uzzi's father that Uzzi would inherit his gold. Afterwards, as is the Elohist custom, it would fall to my sons. My mother's property would come to me, and then to my daughters.

We sealed our marriage before the Lady. Everyone said She was well pleased with us. Uzzi's uncle was a priest, and we also made an oath in the Elohist tent in Zorah. Our offerings there were oil and two lambs.

I birthed four children, a girl Yahida, and three boys, all given Elohist names because of our agreement, Harim, Bara and Yonatan. My third son's birth injured me, and my mother said there should be no more children. She told me whenever my Vulva Blood did not come in any month I should take the Lat Day herb. I always did so, even after my youngest son Yonatan died and Uzzi was fearful, being left with only two sons.

My mother died, and the care of the orchards and the rest fell to me as agreed. Uzzi pressed me to divide my inheritance with my sons. He asked me to give them an orchard each, for the Elohists have little land and so value it greatly.

My Allmothers have held these orchards for over a hundred generations. I reminded Uzzi of our agreement that his father's wealth was for my sons, mine for my daughter. He admitted this.

When we were ten years married, Uzzi asked for permission to marry a girl of his own tribe. I said I would approve it, so long as he remained true to the oath that his father's gold would become the property of my sons, and he would not give any to the children of his new wife. Uzzi agreed, and we brought Nahima into the house. Nahima gave birth to a boy and died. The boy was named Ebed. We raised him in our household.

When we were fifteen years married, Uzzi's father died, and his gold came to us.

When we were sixteen years married, my husband came to me with a grave face. He said the Elohist High Priest had commanded all the men to go to Yarosaleem immediately to see him. No one knew why. The weather was very bad, raining heavily, but Uzzi said his gold would be seized if he did not obey.

When he returned after a week, he was sick and shivering. I thought he had caught an illness because of travelling in the rain. But it was not only that. The High Priest had declared that all Elohist men who had married among us had to renounce their marriages and leave their wives and children.

Uzzi said, "We are not allowed to marry foreign wives, because it angers Elohi. I didn't know this. None of us knew it. It was for this reason our fathers were made slaves in Babylon, because we had angered Elohi."

He wept loudly, saying he did not want to leave me, did not want to throw off my sons. But when I urged him to refuse to obey, he said it was not possible. His gold would be seized, he would have nothing.

We were then in the middle of our olive harvest, and more than half our workers were Elohists. Uzzi was so frightened he refused even to let them finish the harvest for me. He sent messages to the orchards to call them in at once. He said Elohists were required to separate themselves from strangers.

I said, "But *you* are the strangers! You are the foreigners! Your people came here, where we have lived for generations. How can you separate yourselves from us, unless you leave our land?"

He had no answer. But in his great distress, even so sick as he was, he would not lie down on his bed. He began to collect his clothes and tools, while giving distracted orders no one understood, then changing them to others that still no one understood.

I begged him to renounce Elohi-worship. I said they could not seize his wealth if he were one of us. He was already one of us, for he worshipped with me at the Asherah temple much more often than with the Elohists, who had to go to Zorah. But he was afraid to stir up Elohi's anger against his people. He loaded his pack on his mule, took the hand of the child Ebed, and went back to his mother's house.

The workers came to me asking for the day's pay. They were wide-eyed with confusion and fear, for if they could not work for me they would have nothing. Many were couples who worked for us year after year at all seasons, planting, watering, harvesting, and pruning. Most of the women were crying, and begged me, "How will we feed our children, my Lady? Please help us!"

I was too angry to be kind. I said, "It is your god's will that they starve, and you must obey him in that, as in everything."

I went out to the orchards in place of Uzzi, but with only half the workers the harvest went slowly. In two orchards every tree had dropped its olives before we could harvest them. Some of the men came back, in secret, and asked to work again. I told them I would cut their wages to make up for the lost harvest. I said, "That is what Elohi has taken from you."

They wrapped their headscarves in the style that our men do, so that anyone passing the orchards would not see they were Elohists. A few women returned, too— those of our people who had married Elohist men and who were also abandoned with their children. I paid them full wages.

My husband Uzzi took the illness to his chest, and I heard he was laid on his bed at his mother's house for many weeks. In his distress as he was leaving my house, he had forgotten his father's gold, which was hidden under the floor. When his health improved enough to allow it, he came to me, asking for the gold.

I refused. I said that when we married he had promised to give it to my sons. He said he could not do that now because of the ruling of the priest. He said that he was in distress and very needful of the gold because he could do no work, and that the boy Ebed should inherit whatever was left when he died, because he had nothing else to give him. I reminded him that he had confirmed that my sons would inherit when he married Nahima, and he admitted it.

Now Uzzi has at last died from his long illness, and his mother is asking the High Priest in Jerusalem to rule that the gold should be seized from me on behalf of the boy Ebed.

I appeal to the Great Lady and her High Priestess to protect me and rule that the gold is rightfully the property of my sons.

THE TESTIMONY OF SELAMA

Recorded by the High Priestess and Scribe Mar-Yahu

1 both loved and hated him. He was wild, full of fire. His eyes had so intense a gaze that I was enthralled. He was in a passion about everything. Foolish questions tormented him—that a woman would engage in the congress rites with a man not her husband, for example.

In the old days, it used to be everyone's duty to the Great Goddess. I still worship at the Asherah temple on the High Holy Days every spring. I remember as a child seeing my mother go off with her women every month; when she came home, she was bathed and perfumed with that special scent, always in a good humour, laughing with her women about the men they had worshipped with.

My women don't accompany me. They go only to the Diana temple now. Some don't even go there, for fear of the wrath of Elohi. They go to my grandfather's great temple, where there is very little feasting and where bodily pleasure, especially for women, is frowned upon. They call our sacred worship "fornication".

He was an Elohist. A prophet and a madman, one of those whose life's work is admonishing others and calling everything pleasurable 'sin'. He was scandalized that I had been raised without any knowledge of his religion, which he said was properly my own. "You are a Hebrew, why do you worship with Romans?" he asked me the first time he saw me coming out of the Diana temple.

I laughed, and said, "I am a woman, and I worship with women."

He wanted to teach me the right way. I agreed for my own reasons. I knew he was lying to himself. If he had been as honest as he imagined himself to be, he would have kept well away. Instead, he sought to teach me what his god required of me.

I don't know why he imagined that I was interested. Who could love a god who sends men into the streets to rant at strangers, who makes Holy Congress a sin? Even those who are born to it must have doubts.

He averted his eyes every time he passed the statue of Diana Bathing. He said I had to bind my breasts firmly while he was giving me lessons, as if that made *him* virtuous. All men are blind about themselves to some extent, but not all are such wilful hypocrites.

The lies he told! How the world was born not from Great Nammu's spread Vulva, but from the mouth of Elohi, by a word!

I laughed at him, asking him how anything could be born except through a Vulva, especially a whole world. He said a word was the most powerful thing on earth. He couldn't see how feeble his own words were.

He told me that Elohi's real name was *Yahuha*, that it was a secret name. I said, "That is the name of our sacred Lady, only with the word 'he' attached. Do you think you can make Her male by such tricks? A Goddess does not become male by a *word,* whatever you pretend."

That angered him, and he shouted that this had been Elohi's secret name since the earliest holy prophet led our people out of Egypt many generations ago. I replied that

Yahu was birthed and named by the Great Mother even before the world.

I thought he would end the lessons then, but his hunger was too strong, his passion so confused with his religion that I think nothing I said could have come between us.

I said to him once, "All this hot disapproval of congress worship and women would disappear if you once worshipped at the Asherah temple and understood the truth of her sacred rites." But he could not hear.

The Lady won in the end. He was reading to me from one of his scriptures, some condemnation of Elohists who worship at Asherah's temple. He meant me, I knew, he meant to frighten me with Elohi's disapproval.

He was confused, as many are, between Priestesses and worshippers; he thinks that because I sometimes worship at the temple with strangers, I must be a Congress Priestess. Qadeshtu—which he said meant temple prostitute. I pretended confusion over the word. I said, "Qadesh. Is this not a word that means sacred in the old language?"

He said "No," too quickly. Then he said, "That is not what the word means here. Here it means temple prostitute."

I said, "Congress Priestesses are the holiest of individuals. They dedicate themselves to sending the Lady offerings through the pleasure of Her people and themselves. That is why they were called Qadeshtu in the old days."

I think he was shocked, the way one is shocked when one suddenly sees those reverse images that conjurors produce. And that little shock was enough: his guard fell, as if a memory from his own ancestors made him see me in a different way, not as sinful, but holy. I reached and stroked his cheek and neck with the lightest of touches, and my robe fell open.

He was awkward and rough, astonishingly untutored for a man of his age. Nevertheless, we managed to please the Lady between us. But I was wrong: he saw nothing, he learned nothing. Our pleasure made him ashamed and guilty. He turned away from me and hid his face.

I said, "Do you see how twisted the god you worship is, to make this shared pleasure a reason for shame?"

I didn't see him again for weeks. I missed him and the wild intensity of his lectures to me.

And when he next appeared he looked dreadful— thin and dirty, his hair matted, his beard untrimmed, his face burnt black by the sun. He had gone out into the wilds to starve himself in self-punishment and he looked as if it had nearly killed him.

He came back to me. It was the Lady's doing. If he had recognized Her power, understood what it meant, much would have been different. But he could only be with me and then feel shame and remorse. He could not recognize the truth. He could not break the shackles his religion put on his mind. He could only wash people in the river and tell them they were new-born without sin. The state he wished for himself. The state the Lady would make him feel, if he could ask.

He tried and tried to bring me to his sense of shame, to make me confess his god as truth. He could marry me if I pledged myself to Elohi. I would not confess a god that considered my body evil. I told him that his sense of shame would persist, married or not, that nothing could cleanse his mind of its terrible stigma until he renounced his god and embraced the Lady.

And then he began to attack my mother, calling her *harlot*—the Elohists' favourite word for women—because she had divorced my father and married again. He told my stepfather to throw her off as a *corruption*. It was a word he wanted to use to me, I knew that. I was angry. I railed about his hypocrisy. Everyone in the palace knew how angry I was.

So when my stepfather had him killed, he thought he was doing me a favour by presenting me with the severed head. It was all too late then. I had both hated and loved him, but that did not comfort me.

THE MEETING AT THE TEMPLE

Testimony of Mar-Yahu, High Priestess of the Goddess Asherah, daughter of the High Priestess Kanoha, daughter of the High Priestess Delab, descended through four hundred and forty-nine generations from Asherah, daughter of the Great Goddess Yahu, Goddess of the High Holiness, dedicated to the service of the Queen of Heaven. Inscribed by her own hand on Lady Day of Daughter Week of Setanu Moon in the fourth year of her reign.

I woke this morning with the Goddess seed in my womb, from a dream that told me I must perform the rites so that the seed should be watered, and the Lady would give me a daughter of extraordinary holiness. I ritually bathed and my assistant and I prepared the sacred bed with cedar boughs and clean linen and perfumed it with a few drops of our precious patchouli.

I waited for a worshipper to arrive, because it is dangerous now to go out into the street to invite a man to the rites. There is so much unrest. Some of the men who sacrifice to Elohi become enraged at the sight of a Priestess of Asherah. But just as many of them come to the temple door at other times, seeking the rites, as do the Greek merchants and the Roman soldiers and others.

Not long after we had prepared, a man did come. An Elohist, small and wiry and with a face of anger, as so many of them have on seeing me, and my Vulva did not warm with welcome. I told him so, but he was urgent, lifting his robe to show a strong and ready Root, eager for the Work. My assistant Yazbul laughed in delight at such

unexpected size from such a little man, and I felt
Asherah's pleasure beckon.

My assistant recited the congress prayer and showed
him where to place his offering. Then she led him to the
altar. There I made the herb offering, then untied my robe
over Asherah's Vulva.

Instead of kneeling in devotion and offering the Holy
Kiss, he took hold of me so that I could not resist, and
without a word of the litany, no sacred gesture or recital,
no Mouth Worship, pushed his Root into her Holy Vulva.
He quickly withdrew, and his sweetwater spilled down my
thigh.

"I do not defile my seed with such as you," he said.

Never has any man tried such corrupt practice with
me. I felt Yahu's anger, and told him that he was a blasphemer. I ordered him to kneel and give her Vulva the
Mouth Embrace so that the Lady should find some worth
in the encounter, or he would feel her displeasure all the
rest of his days.

But instead, he seized my arm in a cruel grip, cried
"wicked, wicked woman" and dragged me out of the
Sanctuary, through the temple and outside. Yazbul came
after us shrieking dismay.

In the street a group of men waited, two in the robes
of Elohist priests. Several I recognized, including one of
the priests—those who come to me for the sacred rites
only after dark. Their faces, usually smiling in supplication,
filled me with fear now.

"She has been taken in the act!" the blasphemer called
to them, and opened my robe. "See the filthy moisture still
on her thighs!"

A loud cry went up among them. They rushed to surround me, two immediately laying hold of me so that I was helpless. Yazbul stood at the door of the temple, her face stretched in horror, and I signalled her to go back inside.

The mob began to drag me along the street, crying that word they use—harlot. "Behold the harlot taken in the deed!" The stench of rancid oil too many of them had used on their hair caught in my throat.

I cried, "I am the High Priestess of the Sacred Lady! Stand back from me!" And for a moment all stopped. Those closest to me were startled and loosed their grip, and the others stood for a moment uncertain, but too close for me to break past.

Then one cried, "Cover your shame, harlot!"

"Shame?" I put my hands to my breasts, where their violence had opened my robe. "These breasts fed you in your infancy, as the Goddess feeds you from her fields and folds, and comfort you in your manhood, as the Goddess comforts her people! How are they my shame?"

I opened my robe further. "Do you call *this* my shame—my Holy Vulva made in the image of the Goddess's own, which spread to give you life when you were a helpless nothing, and spreads now to take the Goddess's Holy Pleasure with you?"

Then suddenly the voice of prophecy was with me, and I knew that She would avenge me on all of them.

Beware, you men of ignorance,
for She makes you as eunuchs!
Never again shall you offer the holy pleasure rites,

not with your wives,
nor with your slaves, male or female
nor with captive children,
not even at the holy altar of the Lady Herself.

Those closest to me drew back in horror. They do not understand our prophecy tongue, but the curse was on them, and they could feel it. But the one who had entered the temple, his face bloated with rage, pushed forward and again shouted that word.

"Harlot! To the temple with this filth!" He slapped my breast with a blow that made me cry out; and those on the outskirts of the group roared with him so that some found their courage and seized hold of me again.

They dragged me to their own temple, up on the mount, where I had never been before. Men milling about under a long portico stared in curious surprise as they saw the group pulling me past.

They took me along a broad pillared court that was filled with such bustle that at first, as in the Jove temple, I was stunned by the noise. The sharpest sound was the bleating of goats and lambs being led to and from pens, but I heard also the racket of hammer and chisel. People crowded the money tables, haggling as they do in the Jove temple where I go if a worshipper has offered foreign coin. I recognized the painted clay medallions on the wall above that signalled which money could be exchanged.

Several workmen, their faces white with dust, went through carrying timber and slabs of marble with a shout of "Heads!" They passed under an archway that had a sign: "No women or mules past this point." Some were loading a mule's baskets from a mound of broken stone and marble.

We passed a large mosaic of the Roman gods— Venus and Jove and two or three others. I wonder which is worse—to have your sacred places desecrated and utterly destroyed, your holy Priestesses violated, tortured and at last put to welcome death, your most sacred icons degraded by soldiers' shit, by fire, and the hammers of the ignorant, as we have suffered at Elohist hands—or to be allowed to carry on your worship, your temple still standing, with the compromises that hurt most: the blood sacrifice of forbidden animals on your holiest altars, the statues of alien gods in sacred spaces, as we hear the Elohists have suffered at the hands of the Romans?

Men were leading the sacrifice animals here and there, the shit-collectors sweeping up after them. I recognized one collector. Such men are out-of-work farm workers and hire-shepherds who come to the city to try to earn something to take back to their families and instead end up hungry and desperate and collecting manure.

The temples let them collect the manure but pay nothing for the service. They are dependent on tips and charity, mostly from the travellers who come to change their currency and are grateful to have a mess cleared from their path. Sometimes they can sell the manure to farmers with fallow fields, one told me. They share their tips with the sacrifice handlers, who deliberately lead the animals by the exchange tables to ensure that there are droppings in the travellers' way.

These men come to me for the worship rites; they are unhappy, having left wives and children in their villages.

They always smell of goat and manure, and I tell them to go to the baths and pay their Goddess-coin to the bath attendant with a prayer, and the Lady will accept it. Then they return to me, clean and grateful, and only pass their hand over the offering bowl.

They are deeply respectful and eager for the Goddess rites, most of which they are unfamiliar with. Once one said to me that when he had saved enough to go back home he would delight in surprising his wife with the pleasures he had learned from me.

One from a far village—he told me five days' walking—was so taken with Kissing the Goddess Flower that he carried on from one hour-bell to the next. I told him afterwards that the Lady was well pleased with him, and he would surely feel Her blessing, for I had sent up pleasure offerings at least twenty times.

My Allmother told me that on this hill there once stood an Asherah temple that was big enough to hold the whole of the city on the great festival days. But that must have been long ago, for the Elohist temple is old.

Oh, to have lived then, when the Great Lady was worshipped by all! When a single temple would house a hundred Congress Priestesses, when the festivals had five thousand couples worshipping at once, so that their pleasure cries drowned out the music and were carried on the smoke to Her dreams! So the records attest.

The men dragged me (for they would not let me walk upright, instead pulling me this way and that so that I staggered like the wine-drunk) past all the noise and towards a quiet open space where another row of pillars looked out over the city.

"There he is!" one cried, and we moved towards a group standing and sitting around a man seated on a marble bench.

The man was speaking but the mob cared not for that. They pushed through the little crowd and dragged me to stand before him, shouting, "Teacher, teacher!"—a term of respect in their language, but I could see what moved them was not respect.

He looked at them and then at me, and I saw black eyes that were at once calm and alert, and held none of the usual self-satisfied contempt of the important men of the city, Roman, Greek, or Hebrew. He was dark, no mistaking him for a Roman or even a Greek, I thought. His demeanour calmed me, and I was able to take a full breath for the first time since being dragged from my temple.

"Teacher, teacher," they cried again, and then quieted as one of the priests stepped forward. In spite of the high sandals he wore, his head was little higher than that of the Teacher, but he wore their priests' headgear, which was about a cubit high, and at first he seemed to tower over him. The priest was sweating hard, and the hat wilted and tilted over, as they sometimes do in the heat.

"She has been taken in sin!" this one cried, pointing to me with a thick forefinger that was close enough to bite. "Sin" is the ugly word they use for those sacred rites never offered to their own cruel god. I showed him my teeth and he lifted the hand to adjust his hat and fell silent.

Now they all began shouting at once. They lied, saying that they had found me in the performance of Her holy rites, shouting that their religion ordained that I be stoned to death and demanding his approval. Some had picked up stones and bits of broken marble already, and I saw that others were looking about them. I knew they meant me to be their blood sacrifice, here at the temple. Did it depend on this man's judgement?

"What say you?" cried the priest of the melted hat. "Shall we stone her, as the law demands?"

I opened my mouth to tell them I would submit to no judgement of a god not my own, and if they killed Her highest servant, they should fear the Lady's wrath.

But at that moment the Teacher bent to the ground and traced with his finger in the dust the secret mark of the Goddess. Only I and my successor know that mark. I was so aghast that I reeled, and all words were choked in my throat. The pain in my arms as they held me upright was all that kept me from fainting. How did he, a stranger to us, a *man,* know this most sacred of signs? Why had he revealed it to these barbarian men? It was a defilement so deep I couldn't breathe.

But they didn't look at what he signed, did not seem to notice it. Maybe it was too faint in the pale dust against pale stone for anyone but me to see. They seemed bewildered by his silence and fell silent themselves.

"What says he, what says he?" someone cried.

He sat up. "The one among you who has never sinned should be the first to throw."

For a moment there was silence. Then the two who held me let go and they all began to step back from me.

I have heard that when there is a stoning a friend of the victim will join the mob and, as it begins, throw a stone hard to the temple, so that the victim immediately dies or falls unconscious. Then the crowd has to satisfy its righteous bloodlust not with suffering and pleading but with merely heaving stones at a body on the ground.

I had no such friend among these.

I did not flatter myself that any of those who had come to worship with me in the past would wish to ease my suffering, for in killing me they would kill their own weakness.

As the men backed away, Yahu's fury lifted my head and my breasts, and I stood straight and gazed at them. My stomach heaved, and I tasted bile.

The Teacher returned his gaze to the ground and wiped away the sign he had traced on the tile. I waited for the first blow.

I heard a stone fall to the ground. And one by one, then all in a clatter, they dropped their stones, turned, and slunk away. Even his own group dispersed, only a woman and two or three men remaining.

Relief flooded me so that I staggered and nearly fell. I reached for the pillar beside the Teacher, staring at him.

Still not looking up, he said, "Have they gone?"

I said, "They have."

He sat up. "Then you may go yourself," he said. "Don't sin again."

Her rage was still with me, and I turned it on him who was most blameless. "Why do you call it *sin*," I asked, "when if you know the sacred sign you must know it is not sin but a gift of most sacred necessity? A holy rite of worship of the Great Mother that is performed to pleasure Her and keep the fields and flocks fertile."

The few around him stirred uncomfortably, though the woman had something else in her eyes as she watched me.

Elohist women are mostly passive, even the highest born, moving through the streets with bowed heads and bound breasts, their voices subdued. Perhaps it is why the men so hate me and Her followers, who meet them with a steady chin.

He stood up and signalled dismissal to the few still there, and they bowed and left us.

"If I had said, it is no sin, they would have killed you," he said.

My womb stirred with understanding, and I stared and said, "You are a Knower."

How strange that a *man* should be so, and yet it was so. He looked at me as if waiting. I said, "My teacher was my mother the High Priestess, Kanoha. She told me that our Allmothers were Knowers. But many were killed over time, and much of the true wisdom was lost to us."

He heard without comment and still we stood there. No one took any notice of us in the shade of the portico. The noise of the courtyard behind seemed shrouded to my ears.

I did not know how to ask him how he knew the sacred sign. I said instead, "Why did you make the sign?"

He smiled. He was an attractive man, virile and robust, his hair dressed with fresh oil and myrrh. "So that you would not speak at that moment. So that my words would enter their ears and their bodies." He began to walk with me.

We passed back along the pillared walk together. I said, "There are women among your followers." He nodded without speaking. I said, "But your people forbid women to worship." This I had been told many times.

"Not to worship," he said. "To perform certain of the rites of worship."

We stepped out to the street and still he walked with me. I said, "You cannot walk through the streets with me, your people will be offended."

He laughed in delight, saying, "My people are regularly offended by the company I keep. They imagine teachers should only associate with priests and kings."

That gave me courage, and I said, "Those men interrupted my preparations. Come and worship with me. My womb has a daughter waiting. If *you* water my womb, she may be a Knower."

For a moment he was still, his gaze distant. Then he looked at me.

"Do you see it?" he asked.

"It is not a certainty."

He inclined his head and we walked on.

I said, "Still, I will cover my breasts closely, lest their outrage should reach heaven." Then we were laughing together, as if that were a wonderful joke, and I think I will remember that moment as the best laughter of my life.

At my knock, we heard the bar being lifted within. Yazbul opened the door, all a-tremble, her eyes wide with the expectation of horror. When she saw me she burst into tears and embraced me. We moved inside. I sent her to her room, for she was too overcome to assist at the rites.

Then I left the Teacher in the anteroom and went in to bathe away my anxious sweat and the marks of the one who had tricked me, and perfumed myself afresh. I took the coin that the villain had left in the bowl and went into the scullery to toss it out the latticed vent into the street. A voice shouted in glee at the unexpected gift.

The bed linen was still fresh and the scent of patchouli hung in the air, although so much had changed since I had laid down the cedar boughs it was as if a year had passed. I knew that this moment held the power of the future. I knew that no rite I had performed with any man in all my life as Congress Priestess and High Priestess had been as important to the Lady as this moment. I felt Her seed pulse within me. Her pleasure beckoned.

I led him into the worship chamber. I said, "You know our rites?" for if he knew the sign he must surely know more, but he said he did not. I said then, "Pass your hand over the offering bowl."

He looked down at me, a little sombrely, then lifted his hands and drew from his finger a gold ring with a dark lapis lazuli stone and set it into the offering bowl.

"Let us respect the rites," he said. As the ring settled into the bowl, the flame of the torch played over it. It was engraved with a symbol I had never seen before.

We stood in silence as I gazed at it. Then I said, "That is an offering indeed."

He replied, "Guard it well and give it to your child if there is one." My womb clenched and my heart swelled as if with an understanding that I did not understand.

He followed the rites as I instructed him, and I think never has the Goddess been so satisfied through me, never have I sent Her such deep, rich, tumultuous joy, the kind the records speak of as occurring when they held festivals with many hundreds all experiencing this best of Her blessings together. I knew then what they meant when the High Priestesses of old wrote of pleasure that would wake Great Nammu from Her sleep. We lay together in the final posture for a long time, drowsy with the contentment in our blood.

At length he said, "Has the child responded?"

I said, "Yes, my womb is well watered. She is there."

He said, "I would like to give you her name."

So foolish are mortals, I said, "It is the way with us that the child chooses her name." He was silent. Then I felt the Lady chide my resistance, and I said, "Forgive me. Tell me the name."

"Call her *Nekhama,*" he said.

It was a word in their holy language, I knew from the accent he used. I asked, "What does it mean?"

He said, *"Comforter.* If things happen in a certain way, you may one day be asked her name by people who will help you. Tell them this name and show them the ring."

I almost promised; I almost said, "I will." I felt his wish that I should, and yet the words would not come. So foolish can we be, even the High Priestess of the Lady.

I said instead, "The Elohists believe that it is the man who plants the seed?" He inclined his head. I asked, "Is it true?"

He smiled. "It is as true as your belief that the seed is your own." Did he mean to confuse me, or did I just not understand? How can both be true, or how can both be untrue?

He stood up then. In the flickering lamplight his beauty struck me to the soul, and I knew that I loved him more than I had ever loved even my mother. I said, "Will you come to me again?"

"It will probably not be possible," he said. He looked at me as though waiting for me to say something, and I knew that I should ask for permission to join the group of his followers. But a voice in me said that it wasn't fitting for a High Priestess of the Lady, and that people would mock me.

And then as he looked at me, I wondered what use it was to be the High Priestess when I did not *know* in the way my Allmothers had known. Then my tongue was freed, and I did ask.

He said, "A group will meet in the Garden of Olives tomorrow at sundown."

I said, "I will come."

He put on his robe, then lifted his tasselled mantle. It looked almost black in the lamplight, like the lapis stone. A vision moved in me, and the voice of prophecy murmured in my heart,

They will drink your lifeblood
As we drink the Lady's Vulva Blood
as wine
They will take our most sacred ritual
and make it their own

But these words I did not utter.

I felt the firm touch of his mind, as if he were waiting, but he said no more. Then he wrapped the mantle over his shoulder and turned to the door. I led him out through the worship hall and the antechamber and opened the door for him. Tendrils from my womb still clung to him, so that I half believed the child was also his own.

"I will come," I said again. He nodded and went out.

THE LETTERS OF MAR-YAHU

FROM MAR-YAHU TO SHOSHANNA

My dear sister,
We have just had the most strange and disturbing news from Damascus. The Prosecutor Shaul has arrived in the synagogues there, not to arrest our people, but to preach that Rabboni is the long-awaited Messiah of his people! He says that he had some kind of experience while on the road—he was knocked off his mule by a blinding light and heard a voice. He claims that it was a message from Rabboni himself.

It is incredible. But our brother Hatam swears he was present for one such speech. Several men in the synagogue leapt up and called Shaul a liar, saying that he had been the leader of the group that murdered Stephanos. Shaul confessed his presence at the stoning, and expressed remorse, but swore he threw no stone, and only guarded the coats of those who did.

Who can believe this? Shaul has been the most violent and cruel of those who persecute us, brutally beating even the women he arrests and imprisons. Two who were witness to Stephanos's death say that Shaul was certainly involved. Steeped in self-righteousness as he is, he may even have been the one to throw the first stone. That first stone is a stumbling-block, as I know well; even a wild mob may lose courage in the moment.

Shaul apparently did not consult any of our people in Damascus before embarking on his testimonial tour of the synagogues. He certainly knows how to find them—he was going down to arrest them! Several of our people took the risk of approaching him, for who knows what his real intent is? They offered help, but Shaul showed no interest in hearing any of Rabboni's teaching. He only wants to preach about his own experience.

Who knows for what reason he is doing this? I am afraid that he has some dark purpose. Is he spying for the king? The Romans?

Have you heard anything? If so, please send to me at once. Brother Michael who brings this letter will wait for your reply.

May you be safe in the love of Rabboni.

FROM MAR-YAHU TO SHOSHANNA 2

D ear Sister,
We have met Shaul at last. It was against our better judgement, but in the end Barnabbas simply brought him into a meeting in Jerusalem (I was then in Caesarea), and further argument was futile. Many still feel it is a mistake to have anything to do with him, but there seems no way back.

He is a man of great self-possession, like a carpet-seller or a conjuror in a travelling fair. The kind where you walk away smiling and then discover that your purse is empty, or your necklace missing.

In his person he is thin and wiry, with a mobile face, thick, deeply-lined skin, a wide mouth, black eyebrows, and burning eyes that he uses to spellbind. What is behind those eyes disturbs me. There is a rancorous madness in him. He hates women. He hardly troubles to disguise it.

Nekhama was present the first time he was brought in to meet me. She trembled as if facing Death itself, and recoiled so hard against my legs I stumbled. I couldn't warm or comfort her for an hour after he left.

Shaul disdains all bodily love. He is one who sends the Lady no pleasure, nor wishes to. All Her holy rites are *sin* to him. He calls it "renouncing the flesh".

Among my people, in the old days, such men made the Root Offering, so that, knowing no pleasure themselves, they were comforted knowing they pleasured the Lady. Shaul, on the other hand, thinks his disability marks him out as superior.

He actually argues against congress of every sort. "If you can refrain altogether, like me, that is the best and surest way to avoid sin," he said in meeting.

I said, "Best to refrain from congress? It is congress pleasure that brings fertility! If all were like you, the earth would die! You speak blasphemy, Shaul."

He said, "Women should not speak in meetings." This is how he avoids challenge—he distracts.

I almost laughed. "Why should women not speak in meetings?"

"It is the Law."

"Rabboni never forbade me or any woman to speak, so what law do you call upon?"

He cried, "The Law of Moses! Women are in subjection to men."

I was amazed. "But you yourself insist on preaching to uncircumcised Greeks!"

"They weren't raised in the Law. They are dead to it."

I said, "I was not raised in your law. Nor were Diana and Yazbul. Nor was Selama, though she was born into it. We, too, must be dead to the law. Among my people, it is you, Shaul, being a man who never sends pleasure to the Allmother, who should ask permission to speak."

And of course by then the original point was lost. I was a fool to let myself be distracted.

May the love of Rabboni protect and keep you.

FROM MAR-YAHU TO SHOSHANNA 3

I wish you could return to Jerusalem, my beloved sister. So do we all. Shaul's faction grows stronger even as his blasphemies grow bolder, and we miss your calm wisdom. You ask to hear more of him. Shaul is a man of enormous pride who pretends to humility. He fools many. To every newcomer he repeats, and then dismisses as unimportant, his claims to high birth, tribe, and study with a famous scholar, saying, "whatever asset I had, I count as a loss for Rabboni's sake.". He is also careful to mention that he is a Roman citizen. Then he disclaims and says how unimportant that is. That impresses them even more. He is well aware that this is so.

Hearing it all again the other day, I said, "If you indeed count your assets as losses, Shaul, why do you recite the list again to every new member?"

He said, "To teach the futility of pride, a lesson you would do well to learn."

I said, "My pride, as you call it, rests in the truth that I was blessed to hear Rabboni teach, and I listened. Would you like to hear some of his wisdom?"

He said, "Even if I believed that he said anything to you, could I trust a woman's understanding?" Several of the men laughed with him.

He pretends to forget that several of Rabboni's closest disciples were women. Other men are beginning to copy his attitude. Even those who were present when Rabboni said that women, too, should strive for perfection and would enter the kingdom, who saw how he encouraged us.

Worse still, women are becoming subdued during meetings—even Joanna is now too often silent.

He has gone out to preach again. Last week we received a report from one travelling with him in the north. Apparently he is preaching that the "true purpose" of Rabboni's mission was not to teach, but simply to die in order to appease Elohi's wrath towards us all! And because Rabboni suffered such a hideous and ignoble death, Elohi may forgive all of us our sins.

Rabboni's teaching is nothing, the execution by the Romans is all. Shaul calls it Rabboni's "willing sacrifice".

I have written to remind them that Rabboni's mission was to teach us about ourselves and our lives so that we could prepare for the life to come. That no one's death can absolve another of sin. That we are each responsible for our own deeds. If I could believe they would read it with anything like attention!

Do you remember Rabboni saying that true worship required much more than simply saying, "I believe," and that faith was only the first step towards truth? With Shaul the path is much easier—declare that you believe that Rabboni was the Anointed One, and you are "saved". That path is so mindlessly easy that Rabboni would surely laugh at the idiocy, if he did not weep.

May the love of Rabboni protect and keep you.

MAR-YAHU, WHOM RABBONI LOVED, TO SHAUL, WHO NEVER KNEW HIM

We hear that you are now preaching that Rabboni must have *resurrected in the body* because the old records of your people foretold that the Anointed One would do so. You say that Rabboni's body was not taken from the tomb by angels but was physically raised to life again, with all its hideous wounds.

Surely you know this for perverse, wicked invention, Shaul. Rabboni did not resurrect in the body but in the spirit. And that is the promise he gave to us who knew him. That in death we would pass into the kingdom, not be reborn here.

You claim to renounce the flesh. Your body brings you no pleasure even now. Why then do you hope to resurrect in the body after leaving it?

The spirit that guides you is a dark one. Renounce it and turn away from its false teaching. Its goal is the destruction of Rabboni's wisdom.

TO ALL THE CONGREGATIONS
IN PEACE, LOVE AND ABOVE ALL, TRUTH

FROM MAR-YAHU, WHOM RABBONI LOVED

S isters and brothers in love,
I have heard that, some because I no longer travel to visit you, some because I am a woman, and many because one who does visit you warns you against me, you reject my testimony and what I report about Rabboni and his teaching.

I know that Shaul condemns anyone who offers you a different gospel as *cursed*—even if an angel from heaven. Do you ask yourselves how Shaul gives himself the right to say so? Even Rabboni never cursed the angels in heaven.

You have been deeply impressed by the moments in Shaul's presence when Spirit descended on you. But Rabboni warned us often against believing because of such signs and wonders.

One day I asked him, "Rabboni, if signs and wonders do not mean the presence of the Holy, what is the meaning?"

He replied, "Signs and wonders are like the clay that falls on the floor when a potter is fashioning a pitcher. Others will glean the waste clay from under his wheel. One makes a small bowl and puts it to use. Another makes a toy to amuse a child. A third will take up the clay and fashion an idol for himself and others to worship.

"But the pitcher that the potter is making will carry water to the thirsty."

I did not understand the allegory, and he explained,

"The one who makes a small bowl and puts it to use is he who heals the sick and gives the glory to God. The one who makes a toy to amuse a child—this is he who performs wonders to startle and amaze, and gains money or adulation from the amazed. The one who makes an idol is he who lies and obscures the truth for his own ends, using signs and wonders to convince, and he will lead many astray, even to perdition."

My sisters and brothers, Shaul is making an idol for you in his own image.

He advises you against trusting me. But he was not there, he never met or spoke with Rabboni. The things he brings to you are his own invention. I urge you to urn away from the falsehood Shaul offers and cleave to the teaching that Rabboni brought us.

May the love of Rabboni protect and keep you all.

MAR-YAHU TO YAZBUL

Dearest sister,
I did ask Rabboni about Great Nammu—I asked, is God truly a Father? Who then is Nammu, who are Yahu and Asherah? Are they false gods, as the Elohists say? Must I give up my allegiance to those I have served all my life?

He said, "That which is to be worshipped is both Mother and Father, and neither. What we call the divine has sent many teachers and prophets since the world was young, for humanity needs constant guidance on its journey. Those who came before me left a trace of their personal selves, just as I and those who come after me will leave a trace.

"The true wine has been carried in many different cups. What humanity should see and worship in such teachers is the Truth they held and brought to the world. Then there is no *This One* or *That One* but only One."

I asked, but did Great Nammu birth the world?

He said that I had to understand this as a story with an inner meaning. He said, "Stories such as these are like a jar holding oil—they are the means of carrying Truth to those who know how to open them and make use of what is inside. They are not themselves literal truth."

He did not speak of these things to the others.

May the love of Rabboni protect and keep you.

MAR-YAHU TO DIANA

D ear sister in love,
    What you hear is true. Some do now begin to believe that it was indeed Rabboni in the flesh, and that we saw and even touched his wounds.

Shaul says his intent is to convince his people that since the old prophecies were fulfilled in this way, Rabboni is his people's long-awaited Anointed One. He thinks the report of this "miracle" will convince them.

When we last met, I said, "You were not among us to hear, but Rabboni told several of us now present that those who need miracles to believe are weak in faith. You give them what they yearn for, Shaul, but there is danger in that. If you give your own people what will convince them instead of the Truth, what will you give to the Greeks? You know the Greeks love many gods. Will you call Rabboni a new god to please them?"

This put him in a fury. He cried, "You are the infidel who worships idols and harlots in filthy sin! I worship the one true God."

I said, "You make yourself a god. You are aptly named, Shaul, for you are our Sheol[15], you are our certain destruction and the grave of Rabboni's wisdom."

Since then he has decided to use only his Roman name—Paulus. He says it marks his transformation.

May the love of Rabboni protect and keep you.

MAR-YAHU TO THE CHURCH AT CAESAREA
IN PEACE, LOVE AND ABOVE ALL, TRUTH

S isters and brothers in love,
You have been swayed by Shaul's rhetoric to believe the inconceivable. How can one person be redeemed by *another's* suffering, or even death? Surely we are each redeemed by our own suffering, that is why we comfort those in trouble with the saying, *it will bring wisdom.*

And how could God sacrifice 'his own son' as Shaul now calls Rabboni? Sacrifice is what we do to please the Goddess and placate the gods. But if God himself makes a blood sacrifice of his own chosen one—to whom is the sacrifice made? Is there some higher god whom he wished to placate? Or did he sacrifice his chosen one to placate his own anger?

Which of us, my friends, would kill her child to assuage her own wrath towards others who have injured her? And who could expect forgiveness after such a deed?

Rabboni's message was not death. It was love. The last thing he said, when he knew he would be arrested, was, "Love one another. That is the whole Law."

I urge you—do not be swayed by Shaul's fine speaking. He uses words to distort, not reveal, truth. His words make you like the wine-drunk and then he leads you through a tangled thicket until you fall into the pit.

May the love of Rabboni protect and keep you.

MAR-YAHU TO SHOSHANNA 4

Loving greetings to you, my dear sister,
Shaul has now cast his lot with the Greeks, and
given them what they crave—Rabboni as a god. He has
created a *triumvirate* to satisfy even the Romans. He calls
the one of his invention *God the Father, God the Son, God the
Holy Spirit.*

At our last meeting, I said, "The grouping is ludi-
crous, Shaul. Why do you exclude our Goddess Mother?
Where there is a son, there must be a mother."

He said, "Scripture tells us that man did not come
from woman, but woman came from man."

I said, "If your scripture indeed says anything so
foolish, Shaul, and you believe it, it is no wonder that you
are adept at twisting reason into unreason! But Rabboni
told me that your scripture says, *He created them male and
female.* Whom should I believe?"

Shaul then recited the scripture relating that God
birthed a woman from the body of a man.

I couldn't help laughing. I said, "This is nothing but
a dream of Elohi, whom Nammu birthed with all the
consorts at the beginning of the world."

They began to shout. It was mistaken of me. I should
have said that Rabboni told me all such tales are allegory.

They will come in my name and will lead many astray. He
knew it. But who could have guessed it would happen so
soon?

May the love of Rabboni protect and keep you.

MAR-YAHU TO THE CHURCH AT CAESAREA 2

Beloved sisters,
You are divided because you each are swayed by externals. Do not consider whether you like or trust or feel drawn to or are impressed by this or that person who tells you what to believe. Look to the truth.

Rabboni's death is not what carries the meaning of his ministry. It is his life and his teachings. He tried to teach us about ourselves, not to be concerned with Paradise or Sheol or our own salvation.

His last, most urgent message to us was, "Love one another." What love is there in his suffering? He did not suffer for our sake, but because Caesar feared his influence. If he could, he would have chosen to live for our sake, to be among us and teach us all he had to teach. His death did not ennoble him, nor us.

There are two images of Rabboni. Which one is truth you must each decide in your own heart: was he a prophet whose teaching was brutally cut short by our Roman overlords, or was he a god whose father god designed his demeaning death as a blood sacrifice to himself so that he could forgive his people and spare us from eternal damnation?

May the love of Rabboni protect and keep you all.

Mar-Yahu, whom Rabboni loved, to Shaul, called Paulus, who never knew him

You are trying to be all things to all people, Shaul. But Truth can only be itself. It cannot be distorted to fit the hopes, dreams, greeds or passions of those who hear it, and still remain Truth. When you twist Truth to fit their hopes for a Messiah, or a second life in the body, or paradise, or a new god, or men being valued above women, it becomes a lie.

The miracle you pretend—that as "the begotten son of God" Rabboni is also God—draws in Greeks and others in great numbers. But it makes it impossible for many of Rabboni's own people to recognize and accept him. You separate him from his tradition and people, and his teachings from the prophets who preceded him. Only you know why you do this. But I say to you that he warned us against false prophets. He knew that such as you would arise to distort his message for your own ends. And he despaired.

You take personal glory from the numbers that you bring into the fold, but it is easy to sell rotten food to the starving. Such poison will sicken and kill many, and their suffering will be on your head.

I beg you to cease what you do and return home in silence. Those you mislead will join their voices to accuse you on the Day of Judgement, and how will you escape their righteous anger? Your punishment will be severe.

FROM MAR-YAHU, COMPANION TO RABBONI, TO ALL THE CONGREGATIONS 2

P eace and love. My sisters and brothers, this is my last word to you. I will not write again. The danger is great here and I fear for my daughter Nekhama. We are moving to a place far, I hope, from the reach of the Roman soldiers. I commend you to our most loving Divine Parent, and to the true voice that each of us has within.

May Rabboni's love protect and keep you all.

Hymns
and Litanies

The Lady Approaches

Holy Vulva
Sacred Womb
Beloved Goddess
We arc the people to whom [you taught][16]
The ways of delight
You taught us the way of love
Be present at [our offering]
You whom the Kiss pleases
You whom the Root satisfies
Come!
Sacred Vulva who loves the Sacred Tree
Holy…who loves…[17]
Come to us!
....

You whose delight
....

Take delight in our offerings
You who decreed [love among] the people
Approach and witness [our offering][18]

WE ARE THE PLEASURE PEOPLE

We are the Pleasure People
Born from the Allmother's joy
She stroked Her Holy Vulva
The Allmother Nammu [pleasured Herself]
From Her pleasure She gave birth
Our Great Lady gave birth from pleasure
She gave birth....

We return pleasure to the Allmother
We send our joy to the Allmother's [dreams]
While Great Nammu dreams our pleasure
Her joy rains....

Nammu's pleasure is the rain on the...
Nammu's pleasure is sweetwater for the womb
Nammu's dreams....

We send thanks to the Great [Lady]
Who ... love
Who birthed us from pleasure
Great Nammu....

Great Nammu [birthed] love
We are the [Pleasure People]

Hail To Great Yahu

We sing praises to Our Lady Yahu
She brought the ways of pleasure
She brought the gifts
She taught us...
....

Praise to the Lady Yahu
Let us sing....

THESE ARE THE GIFTS

These are the gifts
Of Our Great Lady
....
The congress pleasure
....
Worship and praise
Story and song
The dance
....

Planting....[19]

THE ALLMOTHER NAMMU

The Allmother is All
She is birth and [death]
She is the Great Above and the [Great Below]
She is the world [between]
The Great Lady Nammu is the All
We are One with the [Allmother]
Our love pleasures Her
Her [pleasure] flows in us
We are One in Congress joy with Great [Nammu]
We sing in praise [of the Allmother]

THE LADY ASHERAH

The Lady Asherah bathes in the Sacred Pool
Her consort....

She oils her hair
....

The Lady Asherah spreads the cedar [boughs]
On the bed of joy
She lays fresh linen over [the branches]
She sprinkles the bed with arnu [oil]
....

The Lady Asherah invites her consort
She takes....

IN THE MOTHER MOON

In the Mother Moon[20]
Great Yahu sends the gift of Holy Blood

The women gather
In the temple enclosure
They gather in the Most Secret Sanctuary

Asherah lifts the Most Sacred Cup
The women lift their Vulva Cups
Asherah threads fresh-cut thongs of sheepskin into the Holy Cup
The women thread fresh-cut thongs of sheepskin into
    their Vulva Cups
Asherah fits the Cup to her Holy Vulva
Our Vulva Cups are fitted to our Holy Vulvas
We tie the thongs firmly so that no drop is spilled
Asherah collects Her Holy Blood
The women collect the Holy Blood
The gift of the Allmother to her women
We make medicines with the Holy Blood
We make the Vulva-Blood-and-Salt ointment
We make the Vulva-Blood-and-Honey nectar
The Allmother's gift of healing
Is given to her women

The women give thanks to the Allmother
Her Holy Blood flows in the women
In the Sacred Mother Moon

179

WISDOM

From The Book Of Wisdom[21]

1. The first wisdom is love. Love the Allmother Nammu as She loves you, and love all that She birthed from Her Spread Vulva. This is the highest wisdom.

2. Give pleasure to one another, as the Allmother gives you pleasure.

3. The best greeting to a stranger is a pleasure gift.

4. A woman who sends love offerings to the Lady pleases Her.

5. A man who sends offerings to the Lady through a woman's pleasure and his own, pleases Her.

6. The measure of a man is the pleasure he gives his wife.

7. Men shall be attentive first to their mothers, afterwards to their wives, and always to the Sacred Lady.

8. What is blessed in a man is his steadfast love—for his mother, his wife, his sister, and above all for the Great Lady.

9. A woman seeking counsel of the Lady through the Prophecy Priestess shall offer a measure of oil or of grain to accompany the request. She shall bring the oil in a new jar and the grain in an unglazed bowl.

10. A man who does not ask the wisdom of a woman before acting is sure to err. A man who asks for wisdom and then does not act upon it is bent on destruction.

11. A man whose Goddess Root delights in pleasure-giving, he is a treasure, and his deeds glisten like gold before the Lady. But a man who says "a little pleasure is enough for you" will not receive Her blessing.

12. A wise man studies the sacred pleasure ointments and herbs; he learns the sacred pleasure postures. Then if a woman during worship should say to him, "Take the *panj* posture," or "Stroke my vulva with *nani'a* ointment," he will not prove himself an ignorant oaf.

13. A man who fails to hear instruction in the worship bed strays from the true path.

14. When a woman takes a consort, they should not engage in congress worship with any other person for one year from the day of the sacrament. Then his Root will be bound to you, even though thereafter he may engage in stranger worship[22] a thousand times.

15. A man who has made the Root Sacrifice to the Lady to lie in perpetual pleasure with Her, his offerings of pleasure through the Flower Kiss to the Holy Vulva of Her sacred women will please Her in addition.

16. When a man is pleasured by congress before a woman, and she has sent no pleasure offering to the Lady, he shall take the *bao'u* posture and worship with the Flower Kiss until the offering is sent.

17. A man whose Root is unable to give pleasure during worship shall pleasure a woman with the golden *unna* rod. Afterwards, if he joins his Root with her Holy Vulva to send his own pleasure to the Lady it is well.

18. On Asherah Day of Mother Week let your congress offering be made with those whose spirits are troubled or for whom worship is made difficult by disease or deformity. The wild are tamed, the lame become straight, the broken are whole when they send pleasure to the Great Lady. When you assist in the worship of the unfortunate, her dreams rain bounty on you.

19. If a man asks a woman for sacred congress and, being refused, he overcomes her, his pleasure is not accepted by the Lady. The Castration Priestess will take his penis, but she will not offer it to the Lady but throw it for the dogs to devour.

20. A woman's wealth in sacred objects, jewels, gold, fields, produce, houses, barns and animals when she dies will be divided among her daughters. If she has no daughters, it may be divided among her mother, sisters, and her sons' wives. If a woman has neither daughter, sister nor mother, and her sons are unmarried at her death, her property of all kinds will become the property of the Lady's temple.

21. A woman who sends her joy through women shall at the Great Festival invite a man to water her womb. She shall do this even if she can offer scant pleasure from the rite, for such is pleasing to the Lady. She who hears, let her understand.[23]

22. A man whose joy comes from men let him at the Great Festival worship with a woman. If his Goddess Root does not give pleasure he shall make his offering

with the Flower Kiss. Then the Lady will bless his pleasures among men throughout the year.

23. On the second Lady Day after giving birth, you shall bring your daughter to the temple to consecrate her to the Allmother. This is the First Consecration.

24. Your daughter shall again be consecrated to the Lady on the first Dark Moon Day after her first Vulva Blood. This is the Second Consecration.

25. On Lady Day of Allmother of the third moon following her Second Consecration, your daughter shall be consecrated in the Lady's Pleasure. This is the Third Consecration. She enters full kindredship with the Lady.

26. On the second Lady Day after giving birth, you shall bring your sons to the Castration Priestess with an offering of grain or of oil to make the Foreskin Offering[24]. It is a promise-offering of pleasure to the Allmother.

27. You shall withhold from Root Congress between Lat Day and Izadeh of Mother Week each Moon. Do not allow your sacred Vulva Blood to be contaminated by sweetwater.

28. If you take the Lat Day herb to bring on your Vulva Blood when it does not appear, you shall not make ointment or nectar for two months following. Let your Vulva Blood fertilize the fields instead.

29. If a man is caught in the fields when the Lady beckons him with pleasure, and he joins congress with his ox

or his sheep, he shall bathe twice in the temple pool before he enters the temple.

30. Beware of a man if you say to him, "Let us take the *setar* posture," and he replies, "I prefer to take the *turm* posture." If he says it once, I ignore it.[25] If he says it twice, I reprimand him. If he says it a third time, I shun him.

31. A man goes into the secret places of the forest and finds a honeycomb and brings it, dripping sweetness, to his wife. In the same way his Goddess Root searches out the secret places of her Vulva and brings pleasure to her. He will indeed feel Great Nammu's blessings rain upon him.

32. A man who suckles at his wife's breasts is both son and lover. Her heart will open to him, and she will give him wise counsel always.

33. A woman who opens her ear to the Lady's voice and hears well is a signpost to her people, pointing them in the right way.

PROPHECY

THE LAST PROPHECY

There is no hope for us here.

They are working to seal in hiding all our writings, to preserve them from the Romans, who would surely make a bonfire of them. They believe we will come back "when all this is over". But the Lady has told me that no one now here will return to these places. Many will not even leave, but will die here when the soldiers come.

I do not expect to leave.

Only now do I begin to understand what Rabboni said of the teachers and prophets sent from the beginning of the world, women and men. I know now that all earthly love is the same, whether the ecstasy is of the flesh or of the heart, and that divine love is a distillation so fine and so pure it would kill an ordinary mortal like a thunderbolt.

We are all children of the divine, but none are begotten, nor ever were. I understand that neither the world nor Yahu were born of the physical Vulva of the Allmother. But of the spiritual Vulva we all were, and are, and will be forever. He told me, and I trusted him, but now I see the truth of it. So many years it has taken me, and to what purpose? If Nekhama had lived...but in any case, no one came for her. I have his ring still, but I think nothing came about in the way he hoped.

The Lady has shown me a place and I have secreted all the sacred texts that I brought with me from the temple, for there is wisdom in our scripture, too, as Rabboni told me. I will add this last testimony. Then I will await events.

It was in that place that the Lady (as I must still call her) gave me this final vision. The future She showed me is so dark I dread to believe it, but this I saw:

I saw Rabboni glorified as a dying god, a new Dumuzzi; his dreadful agony at execution lauded, celebrated, worshipped. I saw them selfishly happy he had died in such evil torment, believing it a purchase of their own freedom from punishment for sin.

I saw that his death worship will spread through all the lands between the Great Above and the Great Below, and everywhere it spreads the believers will call pleasure worship 'sin'. They will call pleasure itself evil. They will denounce congress joy.

They will deny the Allmother and all Her works. They will hate the Lady Asherah and Her Sisters throughout the world, among all peoples. They will tear down Her images, burn Her shrines, despoil Her sacred spaces, slaughter Her Priestesses, and forbid Her worship.

They will cry shame on the sacred Blood, shame on the Spread Vulva, shame on its sacred pleasures, shame even on the child that enters the world through that holy portal. They will call it sin to have so entered the world, and instead of our human blessing they will call it our guilt.

They will cry shame on the flesh, even while desiring to be reborn in it.

The most sacred gift of Our Lady—the birth of a child—they will call a punishment of pain inflicted on women by Elohi, who hates and blames women as much for the blessings of wisdom the Lady has given us as for the joys of congress pleasure we offer to Her in return.

Men will despise their own holy pleasure and take guilt even from their desires. They will hate their duty to send worship to the

Allmother through the pleasure of women, they will despise women who joyfully send such offerings, and do all they can to prevent them.

They will call womanhood itself a defilement, and will refuse us entry to houses of worship. They will cry shame on our bodies— breasts and Vulva and even face and hair, and require women to hide their best Goddess gifts from view. They will blind women lest they look at the sacred, for even a woman's gaze will be called filth. They will bind the hands of women scribes, and they will efface our stories from the record.

They will denounce Vulva Blood as impure, call it a punishment on women, and destroy our healing medicines. They will refuse the Lady's lifeblood-wine sacrament as desecration. They will substitute the deathblood-wine of the one I loved more than all.

They will divide spirit from flesh, and pretend it is possible to love the one while despising the other. To love the dweller but despise the dwelling. They will call spirit good and flesh evil, and say men come from spirit, and so are good, and women from flesh, and therefore evil.

They will call that highest of blessings, the birth of a daughter, an evil, and will even kill infant daughters at birth—force wretched mothers to smother them, leave them as food for wolves, bury them alive. This I have seen.

In the place of our holy pleasure temples they will build what they call houses of sin, where the Congress Priestesses are despised and the sacred rites and rituals degraded and distorted. The aim of men who visit such debased temples will be only their own pleasure, whether they engage by the sacred postures or by twisted unholy shapes of their own devising.

She will return, the Lady will return—how could She not?— in many guises, but She will be weak and despised. They will put Her statues in their shrines, but they will not perform the rites for

Her. They will not worship Her for the pleasure She gives, instead they will worship Her as one who has never experienced congress pleasure, never spread Her sacred Vulva in giving. This abomination they will call holy. They will paint Her images high in their cities, again and again, but they will not hear Her wisdom, and always She will be first worshipped, then torn down and sacrificed, as once we sacrificed perfidious Dumuzzi.

This I saw, and hardly believe, but I must record it—they will take knives and razors to the Vulva of girls and women, cut out the Goddess flesh and close up the holy passage so that it cannot spread and can take no pleasure. Women will become utterly divided from the Lady and Her blessings and Her power. When men have congress with such disfigured cripples they will take their joy not from the Lady's blessing, but from the pain they inflict through the tearing of scars that never heal. They will rejoice in this suffering, saying it is the punishment of Elohi for the evil of woman.

When they have destroyed the Vulva sculptures and Goddess icons in every temple and home through all the lands, they will build penis sculptures in gross profusion, and pretend that the penis has a value other than sending pleasure to the Lady.

And last, I saw that they will come to despise not only the Sacred Vulva of Great Mother Nammu but all the gifts She birthed from Her Spread Vulva—the Great Above and the Great Below, and the Earth between. They will despoil sea and sky, the high places and the low, the rivers and the fields, the trees and the animals, because they come from Her Spread Vulva. They will dam rivers and destroy lakes, they will burn forests, they will water their fields with poison, they will pen and slaughter animals in darkness. They will spread melted stone on the fertile earth to prevent Her garden growing. They will walk upon that stone, because even the touch of the earth on their feet they will consider defilement. They will blast forests with burning-water. They will defile all with poison and filth and when they choke and fall sick of their own filth they will defile more. They will do all in their power to destroy every gift which Great Mother Nammu birthed from Her Spread Vulva. They will kill those few who try to honour the Great Mother or protect Her gifts. They will blind themselves to Her suffering and frailty, be deaf to Her many warnings.

Then Elohi will at last be victorious. He will send flood and fire and earthquake and plague without number and without check, and the Lady will be too weak to resist his anger. Then there will come unimaginable desolation by penis monuments of smoke and fire that reach high into the Great Above. These will burn all and everything.

Only then will they turn again to the Allmothers' wisdom, only then will they remember Asherah and Yahu and Great Nammu, and be thankful for the Vulva-gifts we were given so richly. But those gifts will be in ruins, and there will be no recourse. No man's penis will rise and no woman's Vulva will soften. None will be able to make pleasure offerings. Great Nammu's sleep will become death.

This is what I was shown in my vision; I am sure I will never see another. Whatever happens now, I am no longer High Priestess of the Lady, nor the Beloved of the Teacher. All that is gone.

APPENDIX

Appendix I

The Calendar

One very early parchment details the calendar of the Goddess People. It seems to have been copied and translated from an earlier cuneiform tablet. The Goddess calendar may have fallen out of use except for ritual matters as early as the first millennium BCE.

Origin

The calendar was ordained by The Great Lady, The Queen of Heaven, Yahu, and all days are sacred to Her.

The Years

The generations are counted from Asherah, via the High Priestess of the capital temple. Whether there was an actual bloodline from which these High Priestesses were always drawn is so far not clear. The years are numbered according to the year of the current High Priestess's reign.

The Months

The year is divided into 13 moons/months, each nominally 27 days, but with an additional day, called Dark Moon Day, added at the end of each month; effectively a month has 28 days.

The Moon names are still undeciphered. They take the same names as the congress postures, but as these words have so far only been found in these two contexts (also in divinatory texts), we have little insight into any meaning: are the postures named for something like constellations? It has been suggested that for each month there was a preferred posture to be engaged in during the congress rites, which may have been dictated by the prominence of a particular constellation, but there is so far no clear evidence of this.

The thirteen names, from the year's beginning at the spring equinox, are:

> Bunu
> Char
> Atana and Utana
> Turm
> Ashur
> Setaru
> Ha'ow
> Bao'u and Ortha
> Arba
> Naruju
> Upara
> Timun
> Panjeh

THE WEEKS

The people of the Goddess religion recognized only three moonphases—burgeoning, full, declining.

Each month is divided into three stages, called (confusingly) Daughter Moon, Mother Moon and Allmother Moon[26]. A moonphase/week is said to be eight days long, but as Lady (or Yahu) Day is attached to the beginning of each eight-day cycle, it is effectively nine days long.

THE DAYS

The eight days of the week are called "Yahu's daughters"[27] in the following order:

> Inanna
> Nut
> Devi
> Asherah
> Fera
> Lat
> Tanrit
> Izadeh

So dates are recorded thus: on Asherah (Day) in Mother (Week) of Char (Moon) etc.[28] Usually followed by the year of the High Priestess's reign.

FESTIVALS AND RITUAL OBSERVANCE

Certain dates on the calendar are earmarked for special worship. Among the holiest ceremonies is the ritual surrounding the collecting of Vulva Blood.

It is enjoined on every menstruating woman, unless ill, to wear the Holy Cup specifically from Lat Day to Izadeh Day of Mother Week every month, and during these sacred days penetrative sexual activity with men was prohibited, to prevent the contamination of the Vulva Blood.

This seems to suggest that all women menstruated at the same time. This is not an unknown phenomenon in the present day among small groups of women living together, but it is the first evidence we have that this could function on a society-wide scale. But did all women who worshipped the Goddess really menstruate simultaneously, or did some women wear the Holy Cup on those designated days as an empty ritual? We are hoping to find further elucidation of this as more of the documents become available for study.

At the New Year in spring, they celebrated the three- or four-day Great Festival. Great Nammu Day, the holiest day of the year, fell between the Dark Moon Day of the last month of the old year (Panjeh) and the first Lady Day of the first month of the new year (Bunu).[29]

Great Nammu Day saw the community collect at the temple. Asherah and her consort led the congregation through the sacred postures, ending in a shared orgasm that was the spiritual community's offering to the Allmother. One hymn fragment suggests that, like religious ritual today, this involved a litany between the Holy Couple and the congregation.

There are numerous other calendar-specific rites, many to do with sexual congress, in both the temple and the home.

APPENDIX II

WHAT WAS THE SECRET?

I t is possible to see *Dumuzzi's Manoeuvres* as merely a simple precursor to the Biblical story of Eve and the apple. But it may be that there is more to the scripture than the familiar moral tale of disobedience and punishment.

There are indications in several texts that there was a secret once known by women (possibly limited to Priestesses) and actively kept from men, and that this secret was the understanding of the male role in procreation. The knowledge seems to have been lost as early as the first millennium BCE.

If this knowledge was indeed understood by some or all women, the reasons for keeping it from men seem obvious: in those cultures where men did understand it, they began to use their superior physical power to control women. Women were reduced in status and in the end often became little more than property. It seems that every culture in the world where this information penetrated saw a decline in women's power, rights and status as a result. It has also generally meant the imposing of restrictions on women's sexual activity, which would have been anathema to those High Priestesses whose job was to enable and preside over open and free sexual engagement for all sexes.

Is this the secret that Dumuzzi was so eager to understand, and which he was put to death for discovering? A clue may be in the fruit—for the fig, especially when slightly dried, bears a close resemblance to the human testicle. This resemblance would hardly have escaped the Pleasure People.

And a fig contains seeds, a fact which becomes visible only when the fig is opened.

Whether figs were actually forbidden fruit for men or not, it is possible that this scripture was part of a secret codex of which the deep understanding was shared only among women. If the fig symbolized the nature of male involvement in procreation, then *Dumuzzi's Manoeuvres* was designed as a warning to women that the secret must be kept from men at all costs.

Appendix III

I t is not possible to establish with any certainty what is signified by the terms *hur, palla, bral* and *shen*. As with the terms for sexual postures, the words are stand-alones. There is no linguistic indication to guide translation.

The foundation scriptures are among the oldest of the texts. In the translation made around the time of Yahzebul, these terms are not translated. This suggests either that the words had a sacred affect, or that already by the first millennium BCE the original meanings had been lost.

Some scholars have suggested that it may refer to mythological creatures or sub-species of human, such as *fairy, elf, dwarf,* and *leprechaun* in English. Others suggest it may refer to those with disabilities of various kinds. The opinion with the largest scholarly consensus is that, in a culture so centred around sexuality, it refers to variations of sex, gender or inclination.

Whatever the meanings and whoever is represented by these terms, however, the intent of inclusion is clear.

Appendix IV

The Congress Rites

W hile it is possible from the various texts to postulate some of the specifics of the rites of the Goddess people, much still remains unknown. It is clear, however, that there were various levels of ritual worship involving sexual congress: some public; some private; some as spectacle; and some communal.

At the highest and most sacred level was the ritual act of congress performed by the High Priestess in her guise as Great Yahu or Asherah, depending on the festival. This ritual could commemorate a variety of different holy conjunctions, notably Yahu's summoning of a human male before giving birth to Asherah, and Asherah's own coupling with a consort, who in different eras was called by different names.

These rites would have been spectacle; that is, the Goddess and Her consort were on a stage surrounded by the congregation who witnessed the rite.

Next in sacred weight were the great festival celebrations. At these, the litany suggests, what begins as spectacle evolves into a kind of mirror ritual with the congregation performing the sacred rites in concert with the Holy Couple.

Communal congress took place in the temple every Lady Day.

Any woman might repair to the temple or a hill shrine and engage in congress worship with passing travellers or others who had felt the Goddess's call.

Congress Priestesses and Congress Priests were present in the temple at all times, and would engage in ritual worship with any congregant wishing it, probably much as priests today are available for confession.

There were two categories of clergy: lifelong and temporary. As a lifelong calling, both girls and boys might be given to the temple as infants by their mothers, or later commit to the temple for life of their own choice. A temporary calling might last anywhere from a few days to weeks, months, or even years. Those who came to the temple as a refuge from difficult lives could serve in any number of occupations there, including as congress clergy.

As with our modern attitude to charitable donations, it was considered a special virtue to engage in worship with anyone who was physically or mentally incapacitated or in some way unattractive.

When there were no congregants or worshippers, the Congress Priestesses and Priests might freely worship amongst themselves.

Appendix V

The Position Of Men
in the Goddess Religion

It is not so far clear exactly how men were perceived in the Goddess society. They were certainly expected to consult a woman before making decisions. This held true on every level. Kings consulted High Priestesses, while ordinary men consulted their mothers, sisters, or wives, and at particular times, Priestesses.

Men were commanded and expected to prioritize a woman's pleasure when they engaged in congress; it was assumed that they would also experience pleasure.

It is not clear at what age boys or young men were accepted into full kinship with the Goddess — if indeed they were. There is some hint in a poorly preserved text that all boys went into service as Congress Priests for a set period (possibly a month) at puberty.

Among men, Congress Priests seem to have enjoyed the highest status. There were two categories of Congress Priest: intact men who congressed with both women and men, and those who had made the Root Offering to the Goddess. These latter apparently worshipped primarily with other men, although with women they could worship via rituals such as Kissing the Goddess Flower, use of the *unna* rod, and other pleasure practices that do not require a penis.

Appendix VI

the Role of The Castration Priestess

T here are several clear mentions of the term
Castration Priestess in various texts, and it appears
her role was to undertake ritual castration[30] and
circumcision, both of which were practised among the
Goddess People.

Castration was not primarily a punishment. While
it was mandated in cases of rape, where the severed
penis was cast to the dogs (See *Wisdom* 20), castration
was more often a sacrament, and the Priestess pre-
sented the severed penis as an offering to the Goddess
on the man's behalf.

What was called the "Root Offering" was viewed
as an important and transformative rite. The man
gained special status. His virtue stemmed from the fact
that, being in constant sexual union with Her, he was
giving the Goddess endless pleasure.

While some men may have made the Root Sacrifice
out of shame over an inadequate penis, many did so on
other grounds. There is no clear indication as to
whether the choice was ever forced or always entirely
voluntary. It is probable that, just as a mother could
dedicate her young daughter to lifelong service in the
temple, she might also dedicate her infant son's penis.

That the Goddess people also practised circumcision is clear, but whether this important ritual
evolved from (and perhaps eventually replaced) the
Root Offering is uncertain. The motive for the sacrifice

of the foreskin was explicitly to delay a man's orgasm in order to provide a woman with more prolonged pleasure. It was performed on every male child shortly after birth.

Appendix VII

Ancient Beliefs About Procreation

I n the ancient world, it is now clear, there were two opposing theories about human reproduction — from our modern perspective, both one-sided, equally half right and half wrong. For the Goddess People, women were spontaneously fertile by the grace (or seed) of the Goddess, and men watered the fertile womb as rain did the earth. For the invading tribes from both south and north, fertility came from the male seed, and a woman was merely the earth in which a man planted it.

Sadly for women, it was the latter error that triumphed for much of human history. This mistaken view dominated the world, and women, for over two thousand years, until a later scientific war over the same two opposing ideas was finally resolved by means of cell theory in the 19th century.

Since not every act of sexual congress results in pregnancy, and a pregnancy will only be visible weeks or months afterwards, it is mysterious how the theory of male seed ever arose. But its triumph over the more logical views of the Goddess worshippers can be explained very simply — the tribes holding such views, whether the Caucasians from the north or the Habiru from the south, were highly militaristic and dominated by masculine violence. Over the period of their conquests these invaders killed vast numbers of those who held opposing beliefs, destroyed their temples and

way of life, and forcibly converted many of the survivors. It is a remarkable testimony to their spiritual
resilience that the tiny remnants of the Goddess People
still surviving held to their beliefs even as late as the
Herodian period.

That the Goddess People did resist the dominant
theory for so long suggests that it was one of the ways
by which they defined themselves. This might be true
especially as against the Israelites, with whom there
were running battles both physical and philosophical
throughout many centuries.

The regular assaults on the Goddess's shrines and
temples, by priests, prophets and sometimes kings, are
likely to have helped the Goddess People define who
they were, as the Israelite prophets similarly defined
themselves against congress worship. Doing right in
the eyes of the Lord often meant, for the Israelite
priests, not engaging in fertility rites with the Goddess
People. By the same token, it may have been defining
to the self-image of the Goddess People to conduct
those rites in the teeth of such opposition, and similarly
to hold to their more reasoned belief in the self-
determining, all-powerful, all-fertile feminine.

APPENDIX VIII

OLD AND NEW TESTAMENT PARALLELS

F or those readers who are not familiar with Jewish and Christian scripture, here is a list of parallels for the various histories recorded in the Goddess Bible:

- The history of *Rahava and Yanab* has parallels with the razing of Jericho in *Joshua* 2:1ff
- *Judges* Chapters 13-16 (Samson and Delilah) mirrors the story of *Bahloul and Shilah*
- *Ya-Mar's* testimony seems to reflect the story of Tamar, *2Samuel 13*
- For divinely-mandated forced abortion against a woman suspected of sexual infidelity, as recorded in *Arnoan's* testimony, see *Numbers* 5:12ff
- *The Petition from Urus* seems to reflect a situation described in *Judges* 19:22ff
- *Eanna's* story is reflected in the early chapters of *Samuel*
- *Yahzebul's* history mirrors Jezebel's 1&2 *Kings*
- Chapter 9 of *Ezra* provides a background to *Ashdida's* petition (also *Nehemiah*)
- *Selama's* testimony seems to recollect *Matthew* Chapter 5
- *The Meeting at the Temple* reflects an incident recounted in *John*, Chapter 8
- *Mar-Yahu's* letters reflect various incidents recorded in the *Acts* and in Paul's *Letters*

LIST OF ILLUSTRATIONS

Cover: "Nile Goddess" sculpture by Ama Menec. Used by permission

Opposite title page: "Vulva stone", c. 6,000 BCE, Har Issa, Israel. After a copy in private collection

Foundation Scriptures: Goddess, Egypt 2-3rd c. BCE, after a copy in private collection

Text divider, cover, passim: Sumerian cuneiform "Deity", c. 2500 BCE, © Geoff Richards. Used by permission

The Histories: "Goddess Vulva", provenance unknown, after copy in private collection

The Letters of Yahzebul and *passim* "Seal of Yahzebul", c. 900 BCE, Lebanon, private collection © 2023. Used by permission

The Letters of Mar-Yahu and *passim:* "Proto-Aleph"

Hymns and Litanies: "Asherah and consort", tile, provenance uncertain, after a copy in private collection

Wisdom: Canaanite inscription, 10th C. BCE, Gezer, after a copy in private collection

Prophecy: Goddess, Egypt, Predynastic, after a copy in private collection, original in Werner Forman archive, British Museum

Appendix: Sacrifice of a child, tile, c. 1200 BCE, provenance unknown, private collection

List of Illustrations: "Goddess Spread Vulva", icon, Assyrian bronze, after a copy in private collection

NOTES

1 Her paper "The People of the Goddess Scriptures" was read out posthumously at the Bachgarten Fintz seminar in 2019

2 Especially in the translation of the scriptures such as *In the Time Before Time*, it is very difficult to know which word to use

3 Two copies of the Foundation Scriptures were preserved—one in cuneiform, and one translated into Aramaic. This has allowed us to offer a very full rendering of many of these texts

4 Ellipses indicate portions of the text not so far read with any certainty. Substantial portions are still to be recovered

5 See Appendix I

6 This expression seems to indicate "a prescribed period; a long time; an unknown length of time" depending on context

7 No clear meaning for these terms has been established. See Appendix III

8 Dumuzzi is a Mesopotamian shepherd god, also called Tammuz

9 The name in this unusual form, an apparent conflation of Inanna and Asherah, is found only in this text. Possibly an early scribal error sealed in by later copyists, or it may be that the Goddess took on different sacred names at certain rituals

10 See Appendix II

11 In the Inanna canon of Sumer, Dumuzzi was sacrificed because he had failed to mourn Inanna's death

12 The term "Allmother/s" refers variously to the Mother Goddess Nammu, or to an individual's grandmother or ancestors in general, depending on context

13 See Appendix IV

14 The name Yahzebul means "Goddess of the High Places". The OT historians appear to have deliberately misspelled the name "Jezebel" by appending an aleph at the beginning, thus disguising the Ya of deity. How it was pronounced, and what meaning this extra letter might have produced, are unknown

15 The Biblical name Saul/Shaul and the name for the underworld, Sheol, are spelled the same in Hebrew. How they were pronounced cannot be certain

16 Brackets [--] indicate probable readings

17 Three ellipses [...] indicate a lost word or incomplete line; four [....]indicate any number of missing lines

18 The Hymn scroll is among the oldest and is deteriorated. Many of the hymns are lost, most are incomplete. The few included here are among the best preserved

19 The long recital of gifts is almost entirely lost

20 This is the only hymn in the scroll to have survived complete

21 These are selections from a very long list. The complete scroll seems to cover all aspects of life, but the emphasis is on love/pleasure

22 Translation uncertain. It may refer to the custom of engaging with travellers in the hill shrines

23 See Appendix II

24 See Appendix VI

25 This is one of numerous instances in this text (the only one included here) where Wisdom speaks in the first person

26 To avoid confusion, in this book we use the terms Daughter Week, Mother Week and Allmother Week

27 The term is mysterious. Other texts so far deciphered name only Asherah as Yahu's daughter

28 For the curious, this corresponds to about the 10th April in the Gregorian calendar

29 The High Priestess ordained a special fourth day for the Festival every fourth year. This suggests a deliberate method to keep the seasons and the calendar in phase, like our own leap-year day

30 Although clinically it is often used in a more limited sense, here the term refers to the removal of both penis and testicles

YOU CAN HELP US THRIVE

If you enjoyed *The Goddess Bible*...

Please post a review on Amazon and Goodreads.

We are a small independent publisher and reviews are

hugely important to us—and to the author! Please take

a moment out of your day to help *The Goddess Bible* find

its audience.

Love, Nammu Books

https://www.nammubooks.ca
https://www.ashraball.ca

Goodreads:
https://www.goodreads.com/book/show/123237526
-the-goddess-bible

Amazon:
https://www.amazon.com/Goddess-Bible-Ashra-
Ball-ebook/dp/B0BY1JNRNP

30776315R00142